PROCEEDINGS OF THE BRITISH ACADEMY • 109

HENRY SIDGWICK

Edited by
ROSS HARRISON

Published for THE BRITISH ACADEMY
by OXFORD UNIVERSITY PRESS

This book has been printed digitally and produced in a standard specification
in order to ensure its continuing availability

OXFORD
UNIVERSITY PRESS

Great Clarendon Street, Oxford OX2 6DP
United Kingdom

Oxford University Press is a department of the University of Oxford.
It furthers the University's objective of excellence in research, scholarship,
and education by publishing worldwide. Oxford is a registered trade mark of
Oxford University Press in the UK and in certain other countries

© The British Academy, 2001

The moral rights of the author have been asserted

Database right The British Academy (maker)

Reprinted 2012

British Library Cataloguing in Publication Data
Data available

Library of Congress Cataloging in Publication Data
Data available

ISBN 978-0-19-726249-8

Cover illustration. *Henry Sidwick* by J. J. Shannon. The portrait was presented by
students and friends of Newnham College in 1889 and currently hangs in the
College Hall. Reproduced by permission of the Principal and Fellows of
Newnham College, Cambridge.

Contents

Notes on Contributors

Stefan Collini FBA is Professor of Intellectual History and English Literature at Cambridge and is the author, amongst much else, of *Public Moralists: Political Thought and Intellectual Life in Britain 1850–1930* (OUP, 1991).

Jonathan Rée is Professor of Philosophy at the University of Middlesex.

John Skorupski is Professor of Moral Philosophy at the University of St Andrews and has written extensively on J. S. Mill, including *John Stuart Mill* (Routledge, 1989).

Onora O'Neill FBA is Principal of Newnham College, Cambridge and author of many books about moral philosophy.

Ross Harrison is Reader in Philosophy at Cambridge, and has written about both Bentham and Sidgwick, including *Bentham* (Routledge, 1983).

Roger Crisp is a fellow of St Anne's College, Oxford and recently wrote *Mill on Utilitarianism* (Routledge, 1997).

Introduction

ROSS HARRISON

THIS COLLECTION OF PAPERS celebrates the centenary of the death of Henry Sidgwick, leading late Victorian intellectual. Sidgwick was, in both senses of the term, a practical reasoner. Firstly and centrally he was a student of practical reason. He thought deeply and wrote profoundly about what we should do, in a way which still influences people thinking about this more than one hundred years later. Secondly he was himself a significant agent. He was an active reformer, particularly of institutions, and we are still living among the effects of his institutional changes. One of these is the British Academy. For Sidgwick was central in the process which led to its foundation and, partly in recognition of this, the Academy sponsored a one-day conference marking his centenary at which earlier versions of these papers were discussed.

Sidgwick's home institution was the University of Cambridge, where he was the established Professor of Philosophy. In Cambridge he was a great innovator. He reformed what was then called the Moral Sciences Tripos (that is, the system of studies centred on philosophy but also including at that time economics and politics). He reformed the administrative structure, being for many years secretary of the main university committee. He nurtured natural science (and paid out of his own pocket for the construction of laboratories). Above all, he was one of the leading figures in establishing the higher education of women at Cambridge. He was the central person responsible for the foundation of Newnham College, one of the two first women's colleges. Later his wife was an early principal of Newnham. Sidgwick lived with his wife

Proceedings of the British Academy, **109**, 1–6. © The British Academy 2001.

in the college, so if we ask where the philosophy professor was when McTaggart, Russell, and Moore were philosophy students in the man's world of Cambridge, the answer is that he was living in a women's college.

Sidgwick's creations still matter in Cambridge, and in the recently written multi-volume history of the university, the volume on this period takes one sentence to reach his name. It uses Sidgwick as one of two representative figures with which to sum up the tendencies of the time. However, if Sidgwick's actions were mainly for Cambridge, his thought was for the world. He wrote what has been described as the first work of modern, professional, moral philosophy. This was *The Methods of Ethics*, which Sidgwick published first in 1874 and then continued to bring out in revised editions until his death (the last is the seventh edition). It is still admired and taken seriously by leading moral philosophers, and the supreme tribute we pay to Sidgwick is that we engage with him as a thinker and an equal, even a century after his death. He still speaks to us, and how he still speaks to us is the central focus of the following papers.

Sidgwick's *Methods of Ethics* makes a new start in the subject. However, it was not the sort of new start that recognises no previous civilisation and believes itself to be building intellectual palaces afresh in a previously barren land. Instead it is itself a historically sensitive work. The methods which Sidgwick discusses are the methods used by the predecessors he admired, Aristotle, Butler, Kant, and Mill, and its partially historical character is more obvious in the first than in later editions. He works out his position in intellectual conversation with his great predecessors in the subject. History is for Sidgwick a resource to be used in the present, so that historical thinkers are taken to be thinkers who speak to the living, rather than their pastness rendering them mistaken, inapplicable, or incomprehensible. Today Sidgwick himself has the same role for us. He is a natural part of the history of ethics (he himself also wrote a good *Short History of Ethics*). However, he is not merely a historical figure. We need to see him as a part of history but we also need to see what he, as a part of that history, saw. We need to engage anew with a project that places moral reasoning as merely part of the understanding of the justification of action; we need the whole range of practical reason. This has been happening in the last twenty-five years in ethics, which is one reason why current leading practitioners admire Sidgwick. By intellectual conversation with him we resolve the problems of both periods: not only his problems but also our own.

The present collection aims to further this process, and to do it by keeping the balance between history and analysis. There are no papers directly on the history of ethics here, but we get comparisons and placing, particularly with respect to the work of Kant and Mill. More fine-grained, contextual history of this kind would have been possible, and the distinguished historian of moral philosophy, Jerome Schneewind, showed just how much can be achieved by looking at Sidgwick in the context of Victorian moral philosophy as a whole in his *Sidgwick's Ethics and Victorian Moral Philosophy* (OUP, 1977). However, here the philosophical tribute to Sidgwick is paid more by analysis than by history: that is, by direct engagement with the thought itself.

Sidgwick wrote high professional ethics but he also lectured to the general public about practical ethics. As Stefan Collini brings out in his paper here, this was part of what he thought of as his task (his proper activity) as a professor. The description of the actuality as well as the possibilities of such practice (Sidgwick's role as a public moralist) is the topic of the first two papers here; and this is where the collection is most fully historical. Yet one of the presumptions sustaining this collection of papers is that thinking about action and acting on thought should have something to do with each other. The presumption is that study of a philosopher of practice should study both the thought and the practice, so that the history and the philosophy illuminate each other.

If the papers here are classified into a formal academic subject area, they are from both Intellectual History and Moral Philosophy, but they are not presented as if these were wholly disconnected elements (Sidgwick and X; Sidgwick and Y ...). The aim is to understand the man, the thought, the time; and for full understanding we need both X and Y. At the conference which led to these papers, earlier (and shorter) forms of them were presented and discussed. Although the sessions could be classified as one part Intellectual History to two parts Philosophy, in the discussions themselves the two parts intermingled in a way

which I think the discussants found to be natural, constructive, and illu-
minating. I hope some of the stimulus we gained from discussing each
other's papers and from the varied audience (which ranged from
research students to a direct descendant of Sidgwick's brother) can here
be made available to a wider audience.

In a moving short fragment of autobiography Sidgwick wrote
shortly before he died, he wrote that the spirit of the pursuit of truth
with absolute candour between a group of friends was the best thing
Cambridge had taught him as an undergraduate. Sitting in the Academy
that day one hundred years later I felt at times that we were replaying
Sidgwickean practice as well as Sidgwickean thoughts. We were in an
élite institution. Although not a group of friends, we proceeded in the
same spirit of candid enquiry, attempting to fit together thoughts from
different positions and backgrounds. This impartiality, this openness to
various positions, this concern for the 'methods' (in the plural) of ethics is
something that marked Sidgwick. It is what led to his early admiration
of Mill (although, later, Mill too was found to have only an impartial
apprehension of truth).

We also heard Sidgwick's comment (discussed here by Collini and
Rée) that 'I would not if I could, and I could not if I would, be popular.' Sidgwick's thought is more naturally for the few rather than for the
many. It is tough, difficult, full of integrity, but without compromises.
He is a philosopher's philosopher. As such he has gained the admiration of the tough practitioners of our present day. The philosophical
papers in the present collection chiefly concern the hinge of this
thought in what Sidgwick called the 'dualism of practical reason'. I
have noted Sidgwick's openness to different kinds of thought and his
concern to engage in dialogue with his great predecessors. His intention is synthetic: the multifaceted truth will be composed of the best
elements of these different views fused together. For example,
Sidgwick resolved and transcended the leading dispute in moral philosophy in Britain when he started work. This was between empirical,
utilitarian, secular thinkers on the one hand (mainly based in London
and best represented by Mill) and, on the other, intuitionist, Christian
thinkers (mainly based in Cambridge and represented by the Master of
Sidgwick's college when he was a student, Whewell). In the *Methods*

of Ethics Sidgwick succeeded in fusing these two apparently irreconcilable complete positions. Like Mill, he remained a utilitarian, but he did so on intuitionistic principles.

Indeed, utilitarianism was reconciled in Sidgwick's eyes with many different levels of intuitionistic thought. For as well as the lower-level intuitionism of Whewell, systematising common moral principles, there was also what Sidgwick called 'philosophical intuitionism', the higher-level pure practical rationality of Kant. This also was reconciled, so (or so Sidgwick thought) utilitarianism could be shown to follow from pure Kantian principles. For good measure the methods of Aristotle were also pressed into service and also found to deliver utilitarianism (since Sidgwick thought that an Aristotelian style of investigation of the common-sense morality of the day revealed it to be utilitarian). So all this fitted together; all these different methods could be reconciled. However, Sidgwick thought that there was also a non-moral, purely prudential, form of reasoning and that this could not be fitted into the mix. Again he could cite a great predecessor, in this case Butler. Yet this did not solve the problem. To be consistent, reason must connect and be unified; yet Sidgwick thought and feared that it was fundamentally dual.

In the four philosophical papers printed here, different strands of this central problem are analysed. John Skorupski (who has earlier written extensively on the philosophy of the century, particularly on Sidgwick's utilitarian predecessor, Mill) gives an account of Sidgwick's methods, in a way which means that, as he sees it, there is no way of resolving Sidgwick's fundamental problems in his own terms. In reply, Onora O'Neill, a major Kantian scholar (and, as it happens, successor to Sidgwick's wife as Principal of Newnham) analyses and criticises Sidgwick's use of a Kantian basis for utilitarianism. In my paper I see how we may be able to understand the problem of dualism by comparing it to the way in which Bentham and Mill (again, the utilitarian predecessors) treated sanctions. In reply, Roger Crisp (another well-known Mill scholar, who has also previously written on Sidgwick) qualifies and amends my use of Mill, and so of how the argument should be presented. These papers are, as I said, primarily analytical, although they help their analysis by comparison of Sidgwick's thought with that of other major historical figures in Sidgwick's own manner.

Yet as well as theory we also have practice—perhaps the British Academy rather than Oxford House or Toynbee Hall in the East End of London, created by the disciples of T. H. Green. And so to the élitism identified by Collini (and to some extent reproduced in our own discussions). Collini's is a fascinating account; and he has no problems writing about boringness in an interesting manner. His respondent, Jonathan Rée, nevertheless wonders whether Sidgwick is indeed that boring and if, as editor of this collection, I may permit myself a pre-emptive strike, I'm inclined also to shade this theme with a difference. Collini brings out how Sidgwick preferred to work with insiders, and it is certainly true that someone who had one brother-in-law who became Prime Minister and another who became Archbishop of Canterbury could never be claimed to be an outsider. Yet we should remember how he became such friends with Arthur Balfour (later Prime Minister), whose sister he married. This was by the enormous impact he had on him as a teacher (Balfour was one of his students). Partly this is the effect of period. Collini is writing mainly about the 1890s, when indeed Russell and Moore thought that he was rather a bore. However, if we go back to an earlier period, he was obviously a great and stimulating teacher. This is the evidence not just of Balfour but also of two other of the great figures of late nineteenth-century intellectual life, Maitland the historian and Marshall the economist. Maitland said that 'he was a supremely great teacher' and Marshall described him as his 'father and mother'.

As you can see, I do not agree completely with my fellow contributors; nor do they agree with me. There were many methods in our discussions. Nor did we in them solve Collini's problem of the possible role of a public moralist. However, we did find it a mutually stimulating and educational experience; we would particularly like to thank the British Academy for the opportunity and the occasion, and we hope that others will also enjoy these papers.

SECTION I

My Roles and their Duties:
Sidgwick as Philosopher, Professor,
and Public Moralist

STEFAN COLLINI

EVEN BY THE STANDARDS of moral philosophers, Henry Sidgwick showed a striking readiness to use the term 'duty'. And even among Victorians, he displayed an exceptionally strong consciousness of the duties required of him personally. It was, of course, consistent with his utilitarianism to insist that the forms taken by one's obligations were to a considerable extent a function of one's circumstances, including, very importantly, the circumstance of whether one occupied a position which carried with it specific expectations or which entailed some kind of exemplary status, where being seen to meet those expectations and to live up to that status could play an important part in calculating the long-term consequences of one's actions for the general happiness. After all, *the* great crisis of Sidgwick's life had turned on the question of a role and its duties, and in the persistence and scrupulousness with which he attempted to think through the grounds of those obligations lay the genesis of *The Methods of Ethics*.

I am not a philosopher and I shall leave to philosophers the many large and interesting questions concerning Sidgwick's conception of duty and its relation to the nature and methods of moral reasoning. My interest here is, rather, in duties in the plural, not in Duty with a capital 'D', and even then only with what certain of those duties suggest about

Proceedings of the British Academy, **109**, 9–49. © The British Academy 2001.

the sense of public role or identity underlying them (and I am conscious of the risk of slight anachronism in importing the full range of contemporary connotations into the use of the vocabulary of 'role' and 'identity'). Roles and identities are, of course, social rather than purely individual matters, involving structured perceptions and expectations on the part of other social actors (to extend the dead metaphor in 'roles'), and they are, therefore, historically variable and culturally specific. In this essay, I want to examine certain aspects of Sidgwick's public roles and identities and his sense of the forms of activity they allowed or entailed. Part of my purpose here is to try to create a little two-way traffic between such literature as there is on Sidgwick and his milieu on the one hand, and, on the other, recent attempts to offer fairly large-scale characterisations of the development of the educated class in Britain at the end of the nineteenth century and of the distinctiveness of the part played by leading intellectual and academic figures when seen in comparative perspective.

This literature has tended to work with a small range of models provided by studies of distinctive national traditions: I am thinking here of, for example, the work of Christophe Charle on the emergence of 'les intellectuels' in France, of Fritz Ringer on the caste of German 'mandarins', and also of my own work on 'public moralists' in Victorian Britain.[1] Such models have been related to various characteristics of public debate and social structure in different countries, but they have all highlighted the question of the different uses made of the growing cultural authority of the higher learning at the end of the nineteenth century. Viewed from within this literature, Sidgwick proves to be a rather teasing case study: he was a champion of the newer ideal of the university as the home of disinterested research, yet one who

---

[1] Christophe Charle, *Naissance des 'Intellectuels': 1880–1990* (Paris: Minuit, 1990); Fritz Ringer, *The Decline of the German Mandarins: The German Academic Community 1890–1933* (Cambridge, Mass.: Harvard University Press, 1969); Stefan Collini, *Public Moralists: Political Thought and Intellectual Life in Britain, 1850–1930* (Oxford: Oxford University Press, 1991). There have now been several attempts to address these models in an explicitly comparative perspective: see, for instance, Christophe Charle, *Les Intellectuels en Europe au XIXe siècle: Essai d'histoire comparée* (Paris: Seuil, 1996); Marie-Christine Granjon, Nicole Racine, and Michel Trebitsch (eds), *Histoire comparée des intellectuels* (Paris: IHTP, 1997).

worked to involve the university in a wide range of practical and vocational activities; he was an exemplar of the new breed of academic specialists, yet one who retained in some settings the imperial ambitions of the generalist; and he was a figure intimately connected with the political world of his day yet who none the less largely abstained from participation in public debate.

In exploring these complexities, I shall here be concentrating on the latter part of Sidgwick's career, essentially the 1880s and, more particularly, the 1890s. I do so for two main reasons. One is that in Sidgwick's case philosophical and scholarly attention has naturally been concentrated on *The Methods of Ethics* and, largely as a consequence of that, on the earlier stages of his career in the 1860s and 1870s, especially the relation between his religious crisis and the development of his moral philosophy. That period, I would agree, was when Sidgwick's thinking and writing were in some ways at their most interesting, but to understand his role as a public figure, even to some extent as a representative figure, we have to turn to the period when his reputation and institutional influence were at their highest.

The other reason for concentrating on this period is that the issues I am addressing about the cultural authority of the higher learning and the public roles of the academic can only properly be formulated for the period *after* the reform of the ancient universities in the 1860s, the founding of the new civic universities in the 1870s, and the beginnings of specialised professional associations and journals in the 1870s and 1880s. Partly as a consequence of this, the literature (such as it is) on the appearance or non-appearance of intellectuals in Britain has focused on the closing decades of the century, when, it is argued, there developed for the first time a sense of belonging to a separate intellectual stratum in society.[2] By looking in more detail at this relatively neglected phase of Sidgwick's work and career, I hope also to contribute to our understanding of the validity and limits of some of the familiar generalisations about the historical role of intellectuals in British culture. I shall begin, therefore, with a brief exploration of

[2] See, in particular, T. W. Heyck, *The Transformation of Intellectual Life in Victorian England* (London: Croom Helm, 1982), esp. 'Conclusion'.

Sidgwick's conception of his roles as philosopher and professor, and I shall then offer a slightly more extended characterisation of the ways in which he did or did not bring these roles to bear in participating in a broader public sphere. Since this touches on features of Sidgwick's work about which I have written elsewhere, there are aspects of his contribution which I shall ignore or refer to only in passing, especially his two major publications from this period, *The Principles of Political Economy* (1883) and *The Elements of Politics* (1891).[3]

1. *Professing philosophy*

A. J. Ayer once divided philosophers into 'pontiffs' and 'journeymen', contrasting the soaring metaphysical ambition of the former group with the (ostensibly) modest analytical aims of the latter.[4] It may be no less fruitful to think of a contrast of this type as also representing a dividedness of aim within individual philosophers. Certainly, one of the most interesting features of Sidgwick's self-conception here is the way he oscillated between, on the one hand, appearing to take all of human knowledge as his legitimate domain, and, on the other, speaking of philosophy as a strictly specialised activity only to be cultivated by the unhappy few. Some of his set-piece declarations about philosophy, insisting on its almost limitless scope, can sound decidedly 'pontifical'. 'I regard philosophy ... as the study which "takes all knowledge for its province"', as he put it on one occasion; 'as philosophers we aim at knowledge of the whole'. Or again: 'I regard the harmonising of different sciences and studies as the special task of philosophy.' And of course this embraced the whole field of practical reason as well: only,

---

[3] See my 'The ordinary experience of civilized life: Sidgwick's politics and the method of reflective analysis', in Bart Schultz (ed.), *Essays on Henry Sidgwick* (Cambridge: Cambridge University Press, 1992), 333–67. That essay is a slightly revised and extended version of Chapter 9 of Stefan Collini, Donald Winch, and John Burrow, *That Noble Science of Politics: A Study in Nineteenth-Century Intellectual History* (Cambridge: Cambridge University Press, 1983), 277–307.

[4] A. J. Ayer, 'The claims of philosophy' (1947), in *The Meaning of Life and Other Essays*, ed. Ted Honderich (London: Weidenfeld and Nicolson, 1990), 1–3.

as he put it in 1899, by combining the study of the ideal and the actual can we 'hope to attain that wider view which belongs to philosophy as distinguished from science; from which we endeavour to contemplate the whole of human thought—whether concerned with ideas or with empirical facts—as one harmonious system'.[5]

I shall return to the question of quite what relation to other disciplines this entailed within the increasingly specialised university, but here I want first to touch on Sidgwick's conception of the method appropriate to this potential meta-discipline. Philosophy, as he put it in lectures given in the 1890s and published posthumously, 'uses primarily what I may call the Dialectical Method, i.e. the method of reflection on the thought which we all share, by the aid of the symbolism which we all share, language'. He argued that philosophical analysis should seek to define terms '*as far as possible* in conformity with common usage', and even though this was not an entirely straightforward matter since common usage is often confused, 'still, I think that here and in other cases we may find distinctions, vaguely and imperfectly recognised in ordinary discourse, which when made clear and explicit will furnish the required definitions'.[6] It is the effect of transposing this method from the domain of philosophy to the necessarily more approximate world of public debate that is of interest here. Sidgwick more than once declared his belief that this method was particularly valuable in subjects that were 'so full of controversy', for on his view controversy 'usually implies mutual misunderstanding among thinkers', and the philosophical clarification of terms could avoid much of this. But the danger, when dealing with practical rather than purely philosophical matters, was that 'controversy' could then too readily be assumed to arise purely out of conceptual muddle rather than out of genuine and irreconcilable differences in experience of the world.

The interesting tension in Sidgwick's position here lay in his attempts to balance a belief in the larger utility of the method of philosophical analysis with his conviction that the serious pursuit of

[5] HS, *Philosophy, Its Scope and Relations* (London: Macmillan, 1902), 10; HS, 'The relation of ethics to sociology' (1899), in *Miscellaneous Essays and Addresses* (London: Macmillan, 1904), 266, 249.

[6] *Philosophy*, 49, 3–4.

philosophy as a discipline was of its nature likely to be confined to a small circle of adepts. We may here refer to a remark he made at an earlier stage of his career when writing to his mother about his newly published *The Methods of Ethics:* 'I don't expect the "general public" to read much of my book. In fact the point of it rather is that it treats in a technical and precise manner questions which are ordinarily discussed loosely and popularly.'[7] Here he not only accepts that to treat a question 'in a technical and precise manner' is *ipso facto* to withdraw it from the sphere of 'the general public's' attention, but he appears to take some pride in this consequence. And indeed, even within the university he seemed to wish to restrict rather than to expand the numbers of those who should be encouraged to pursue serious philosophical studies.

The most extended of Sidgwick's own reflections on his position as a teacher of philosophy came in his journal entry in December 1884 following the outspoken criticism of his 'failure' in this capacity by his former pupil and present colleague, Alfred Marshall. Marshall had accurately, if unkindly, focused on Sidgwick's efforts to

> give a wretched handful of undergraduates the particular teaching that they required for the Moral Sciences Tripos. He contrasted my lecture-room, in which a handful of men are taking down what they regard as useful for examination, with that of [T.H.] Green, in which a hundred men—half of them B.A.'s—ignoring examinations, were wont to hang on the lips of the man who was sincerely anxious to teach them the truth about the universe and human life.

With characteristic mildness, Sidgwick's reflection begins: 'I was much interested by this letter', and he went on to analyse his own view of 'the causes of my academic failure—I mean my failure to attract men on a large scale'. By means of a quotation from Bagehot on Clough, he indirectly sketched his own character and views, especially their unillusioned realism. But this meant, he acknowledged, that he had no uplifting message to give about a world that he regarded with considerable irony. He reflected that this unillusioned view did not make him personally unhappy,

---

[7] HS to his mother, 28 Dec. 1874; Sidgwick Papers, Trinity College, Cambridge, Add Mss c. 99., f. 180 (this letter is also quoted in Collini, 'Ordinary experience', 335–6).

but, feeling that the deepest truth I have to tell is by no means 'good tidings', I naturally shrink from exercising on others the personal influence which would make men [resemble] me as much as men more optimistic and prophetic naturally aim at exercising such influence. Hence as a teacher I naturally desire to limit my teaching to those whose bent or deliberate choice is to try to search after ultimate truth; if such come to me, I try to tell them all I know; if others come with vaguer aims, I wish if possible to train their faculties without guiding their judgements. I would not if I could, and I could not if I would, say anything which would make philosophy—my philosophy—popular.[8]

To which it is, of course, hard not to reply, 'You should be so lucky!' As a philosopher, Sidgwick's chief problem was hardly an excessive popularity. Students of *The Methods of Ethics* will, incidentally, notice that this passage hints at the question of keeping esoteric truths from the masses which also surfaces in his account of the utilitarian method of moral reasoning, here suggesting that most students may best be left undisturbed in their animating illusions. But although the passage concentrates on not having an ethical system to teach, it does also represent Sidgwick's wider view of the aim of teaching philosophy, especially to those who come to it with 'vaguer aims', namely, the goal of 'train[ing] their faculties without guiding their judgements'.

There would not nowadays be anything strikingly scandalous in suggesting that, not just in his actual teaching but also in his deployment of his philosophical method more generally, Sidgwick sought to 'guide [his readers'] judgements' rather more than he lets on. I have discussed elsewhere the way in which, in Sidgwick's hands at least, the 'method of reflective analysis' told in a conservative direction.[9] I want here to consider from another angle the more specific question of what there was, as it were, 'left' for the moral philosopher to do in society once he had concluded that he could arrive at no wholly coherent and satisfying account of first principles. As he had put it in a letter as early as 1873: 'I think the contribution to the *formal* clearness and coherence of our ethical thought which I have to offer is just worth giving: for a

---

[8] HS, journal entry 22 Dec. 1884; in A. and E. M. Sidgwick, *Henry Sidgwick, A Memoir* (London: Macmillan, 1906), 394–6 (hereafter cited as *Mem*).
[9] See fn. 3 above.

few speculatively-minded persons—very few. And as for all practical questions of interest, I feel as if I had now to begin at the beginning and learn the ABC.'[10] In the later phase of his career, 'practical questions' were indeed what Sidgwick concentrated his energies on, though he still did so, of course, as one who brought his philosopher's tool-kit with him.

It must be said that Sidgwick was not always so equable about his role as a professor of philosophy as his response to Marshall may, at least on the surface, suggest. He constantly worried whether he had anything positive to teach, and as Bart Schultz observes: 'The problem went beyond that of meeting (or giving a reasoned justification for failing to meet) the institutional expectations of his role.'[11] Indeed, the 'institutional expectations of his role' were no merely external matter for Sidgwick. In the late 1880s, in particular, he experienced an inner crisis about whether he could really continue to profess moral philosophy if he did not have some kind of positive system to teach, and he even considered, or at least spoke as though he were really considering, resigning his chair (at other times he had flattered himself that although his intellectual position was an uncomfortable one: '[I] take it as a soldier takes a post of difficulty'[12]).

This crisis was partly provoked by his concluding, as he was to do more than once thereafter, that psychical research was not going to yield incontrovertible evidence of the existence of the individual after death, the necessary postulate of a coherent ethical theory. 'Soon, therefore, it will probably be my duty as a reasonable being—and especially as a professional philosopher—to consider on what basis the human individual ought to construct his life under these circumstances.'[13] Even if it could be said that, in practice, moral behaviour would take care of itself, 'my special business is not to maintain morality *somehow*, but to establish it logically as a reasoned system', and this he had concluded in *The Methods of Ethics* could not now be done. 'Am I', he therefore asked himself, 'to use my position—and draw my salary—for

[10] HS to H. G. Dakyns, Feb. 1873; *Mem*, 277.
[11] Schultz, *Essays on Sidgwick*, 44.
[12] HS to his sister, 10 June 1881; *Mem*, 354.
[13] HS, journal entry 28 Jan. 1887; *Mem*, 466–7.

teaching that Morality *is* a chaos from the point of view of Practical reason?'[14]

It is perhaps not surprising that the conscientious Sidgwick should have been more troubled than most by the demands of 'my station and its salary', but in considering him in the terms provided by the recent literature on the professionalisation of academic careers in the late nineteenth century, it is interesting to probe into his anxiety a little more closely. After all, there was no question of his either failing to teach his subject in a systematic and objective manner nor of his failing to contribute to the scholarly literature of his discipline, the two activities that had come to be recognised as the defining obligations of the academic career. Sidgwick's worry was that he did not have a *positive* moral system to recommend. The complexities of this anxiety came out in a later reflection on his dilemma about 'the tenability of my position here as a teacher of ethics'. He elaborated a contrast between the position of a professor of theology and a professor of 'any branch of science'. The latter is simply obliged to discover and communicate such truths as he finds the evidence will support 'whether favourable or not to the received doctrines'; but 'a Professor of Theology, under the conditions prevailing in England at least, is expected to be in some way constructive; if not exactly orthodox, at any rate he is expected to have and to be able to communicate a rational basis for some established creed and system'. Sidgwick's working intuition at this point was that 'Ethics seems to me intermediate between Theology and Science regarded as subjects of academic study and profession.'[15]

From the point of view of 'professionalisation', there is an interestingly 'impure' conception of the role of a professor at work here. The professor of theology is in some way constrained by the views of those outside the university (by churches and their members, roughly speaking), or even, in a more sophisticated version, constrained by the fact that his subject is in some sense *constituted* by beliefs shared with such others, whereas the professor of science enjoys the autonomy

---

[14] HS, journal entry 16 Mar. 1887; *Mem*, 472.
[15] HS, journal entry 8 Apr. 1888; *Mem*, 484–5.

accorded to a professional group with its own internal criteria of propriety. But it is not so clear whose beliefs the professor of moral philosophy is expected to share or confirm; one is left wondering whether the implication is—to return to the categories of *The Methods of Ethics*—that the professor is actually *obliged* to find a reasoned basis for 'common-sense morality'. It is noticeable that in the quoted passage the professor of science is exonerated from having to endorse 'the *received* doctrines' and that the professor of theology has to find a basis for 'some *established* creed and system' (my italics). According to the restrictive conception of the role of the professor of moral philosophy implicit in these remarks, it would seem that a Nietzsche no less than a Sidgwick ought to feel obliged to look for another job.

Sidgwick, of course, did not look for another job, but he did in some ways re-define his role. At times he felt he was in the position of the 'philosopher who has philosophised himself into a conviction of the unprofitableness of philosophy. He must do something else.'[16] Sidgwick did not altogether 'do something else', but it is noticeable, I think, that in the final phase of his life he increasingly concentrated on a variety of more practical issues, partly at the expense of the enquiry— the, for him, depressingly inconclusive enquiry—into the first principles of ethics. Thus, in this period Sidgwick appeared to live with a kind of two-tier professional identity. In private or in the company of a few devoted seekers after truth, he could give himself unreservedly to enquiry into fundamental questions; but in public, or among that large class of persons who had 'vaguer aims', he served more as the medical officer, inoculating them against the contagious diseases they were likely to encounter while serving in the jungle of practical life. Philosophy's role could appear in practice to be limited to that of removing (other people's) confusions, and here one is tempted to adapt Churchill's famous remark about Attlee to say that in Sidgwick's hands philosophy was a modest enterprise with much to be modest about. But we have long been familiar with those apparently modest descriptions of philosophy's role as that of an 'under-labourer' and so on which

[16] HS, journal entry 14 Apr. 1887; *Mem*, 475.

actually express imperial intellectual ambitions, and, as we shall see, even in this final period Sidgwick could on occasion assign philosophy a not insignificant public role.

2. *The university in society*

We can come at this question of roles by another route by considering Sidgwick's efforts to enhance the standing of the university in society. As we know, he expended an enormous amount of time and energy, from the 1860s right through to the end of his life, in attempting to reform his own university, partly by ensuring that its status and endowments were deployed to further the ends of learning and research, partly by expanding and modernising its curriculum, partly by helping to establish the conditions for an autonomous academic profession, working always to free it equally from religious control and from indefensible idleness. (Within Cambridge, as his wife's biographer recalls, Sidgwick the zealous reformer was thought 'charming, but not quite "safe"'.[17] Few things can convey a more vivid sense of the conservatism and conventionality of late nineteenth-century Cambridge than to imagine it as filled with people capable of thinking Sidgwick 'not quite "safe"'.) In the early 1870s he gave his support to, and wrote a large number of reviews for, Appleton's new journal, *The Academy*, which aimed to promote 'the endowment of research' and to bring to the discussion of a wide range of scholarly topics a scientific rigour not found in the periodicals of general culture.[18] Within philosophy he worked to further professional cooperation and publication, not least by supporting the founding of *Mind* in 1876, and indeed financing it out of

[17] Ethel Sidgwick, *Mrs Henry Sidgwick, a Memoir (1845–1936)* (London: Sidgwick and Jackson, 1938), 62.

[18] See Diderick Roll-Hansen, *'The Academy' 1869–1879: Victorian Intellectuals in Revolt* (Copenhagen, 1957). One should not, however, conclude that this was wholly a matter of 'withdrawing' from public debate: consider Mark Pattison's remark in 1882 that the journal was a means towards 'a great public end: that, namely, of bringing the knowledge latent in the community to the top, and giving it more control of the conduct of the affairs of the community'; quoted in Heyck, *Transformation*, 216.

his own pocket from 1892. These measures were also aimed at making a sharper separation between serious philosophical enquiry and general literary culture.[19] His election to the Knightbridge Chair at Cambridge in 1883 was in some ways more a confirmation of an already acknowledged local pre-eminence than a translation to a new sphere, but he was, as one contemporary described him, an exceptionally conscientious professor, with a more strenuous conception of the duties of the post than some his contemporaries were altogether comfortable with.[20] The position and its status mattered to him, and, as I have remarked elsewhere, 'the title "Professor" became as constitutive a part of his public identity as the name of his diocese is of a bishop's'.[21] And of course, in a volume published under present auspices, we do not need to be reminded that he was in effect the prime mover in the discussions that led, shortly after his death, to the founding of the British Academy.[22]

These enterprises may all be seen as part of what is loosely termed the 'professionalisation' of academic life in the closing decades of the nineteenth century. This description, however, risks misrepresenting Sidgwick's concern during this period, a concern which may be better illustrated by a couple of passing references in his private reflections. One small indication of his sense of the figure the academic should be expected to cut in public affairs comes in a passage in his journal which was omitted from the version published in the *Memoir* (presumably because the person referred to was still alive). It dates from August 1885, as part of an assessment of James Stuart, a fellow professor in Cambridge since 1875 and Fawcett's successor as Liberal MP for

---

[19] Similarly, in writing in 1879 to his former pupil (and present brother-in-law) Arthur Balfour about the latter's forthcoming *A Defence of Philosophic Doubt*, he counselled against having quotations on the title-page from Leslie Stephen as 'he is only a philosophical litterateur—has no recognized position as a philosopher'. HS to A. J. Balfour, 15 May 1879; Balfour Papers, B.L. Add Mss 49832., f. 24.

[20] According to Henry Jackson, recalling Sidgwick's attempts in the 1880s to get the General Board at Cambridge to define the duties of professors: 'Himself a professor, and a *very* conscientious one, he took a large and generous view of the work which a professor should be expected to do. The professors, however, resented the proposed regulations' (*Mem*, 375).

[21] Collini, 'Ordinary experience', 336–7.

[22] See Collini, *Public Moralists*, ch. 1.

Hackney in 1884. Having praised Stuart's good qualities, Sidgwick went on:

> It is rather a pity, though, that he has an academic position, since his treatment of political questions is defective in just the respects where an academic person ought to be strongest: he does not exactly know on what parts of his subject there are accepted theories and systematic methods of reasoning, which an educated person ought at any rate to show adequate knowledge of, even if he intends to banish them to Jupiter or Saturn.[23]

Sidgwick's regret here seems to be that Stuart's public display of ignorance is indirectly damaging to the authority in the public sphere of persons holding 'academic positions' in general, though it is interesting to see how far this connects in his mind with the conviction that in politics there really were 'accepted' theories and 'systematic' methods of reasoning (roughly corresponding, we might surmise, to his *Principles of Political Economy* and *Elements of Politics* respectively). Some knowledge of theories and methods of these kinds, in other words, might be especially expected from persons holding academic positions (even if they then went on to disagree with or dismiss them), though it seems only fair to Stuart to point out that the Chair he held was in 'Mechanical Sciences'.[24]

An indication of another aspect of Sidgwick's concern with the public standing of universities is provided by his reflection on the occasion in 1888 when Cambridge gave honorary degrees to a clutch of current politicians. The date is important, since this was in the immediate aftermath of the Home Rule split, and political opinion in the university was still deeply divided. Personally, Sidgwick took some pleasure in the occasion, not only because three of the figures so honoured were his wife's uncle, brother, and brother-in-law (Salisbury, Balfour, and

---

[23] HS, journal entry 24 Aug. 1885; Sidgwick Papers, Trinity, Add Mss, c. 97., f. 25.

[24] It should also be said that Sidgwick could entertain parallel anxieties about politicians where 'accepted theories' were concerned, for example his remark when Randolph Churchill was appointed to the Treasury in 1886 that because he was 'wholly ignorant of political economy ... there is a danger of his bringing out some utter nonsense in arguing on Money or Trade, which will discredit the government' (HS to Lady Frances Balfour, 30 July 1886; *Mem*, 453).

the physicist Lord Rayleigh), but also because the leading honorands were persuaded to grace a social occasion at the fledgling Newnham College. Still, the scrupulous Sidgwick recognised that giving degrees at this delicate juncture to, among others, Salisbury, Balfour, and Goschen 'was, by irate Gladstonians, regarded as a demonstration on the Unionist side', and the occasion prompted him to confide to his journal his more austere conception of the public function of a centre of learning: 'I think ... that a university ought to give no honorary degrees except for merit that it is professionally competent to recognize, i.e. for eminence in science and learning.'[25]

This sensitivity to the public perception of the intellectual authority of universities frequently surfaces in Sidgwick's writings and correspondence. For example, when in 1886 Montagu Butler, the socially well-connected Headmaster of Harrow, was appointed Master of Trinity, Sidgwick, despite his personal regard for Butler, recorded his feeling of 'depression and dissatisfaction at the snub given to academic work', that is, to his belief that such positions within a university should reflect achievement in systematic intellectual enquiry rather than public standing of other kinds.[26] At the same time, Sidgwick can appear ambivalent about how far this intellectual authority should be deployed in the wider public sphere. Here it is important to remember the changed position of the universities by the end of the century: in the 1860s, the defence of free enquiry had involved campaigning against ecclesiastical, if not directly political, control, whereas by 1900 it could seem that a more pressing way of protecting the status of disinterested scholarship was to abstain from direct participation in public debate altogether.

Sidgwick manifested a comparable ambivalence about the related question of specialisation. His conception of the virtues of systematic scientific enquiry entailed welcoming the advances in specialisation so marked in his own lifetime, but at the same time he, naturally, also expressed reservations about them. In 1897, for example, he observed that 'the development of all sciences and studies' had 'driven English

[25] HS, journal entry 11 June 1888; *Mem*, 489–90.
[26] HS, journal entry 1 Nov. 1886; *Mem*, 460.

university education' far away from Newman's ideal of a common, unifying element to the whole syllabus. 'This has been more or less the case everywhere; but—to my regret I confess—it has been most prominently the case' in Cambridge. In the same address he also pondered the question whether 'the specialist' could be 'a man of culture', answering in the negative 'so far as he is a mere specialist'. On this score, therefore, it was necessary to find ways 'to maintain, in spite of the increasing specialisation inevitably forced on us by the growth of knowledge, our intellectual interests and sympathies in due breadth and versatility'.[27] Of course, a public discourse in which 'character' so often outranked 'intellect' tended to assign particular value to ideals of 'breadth and versatility'. Certainly, Sidgwick's even-handedness contrasts with the more whole-hearted defence of the specialist being developed at exactly the same time by Émile Durkheim. In the more politicised debates surrounding the reform of the university in Third Republic France, Durkheim polemicised vigorously against the cultural role of the 'men of letters', dismissed as mere dilettantes, arguing that the specialised scholar had developed disciplined faculties of reason by virtue of his scientific training which made his judgement ethically superior to the flabby generalities of the dilettante. Among the many relevant differences between Sidgwick and Durkheim in this regard, one may note the former's greater tenderness for the Comtean ideal of the coordinating power of philosophy compared to Durkheim's emphatic endorsement of the autonomy of each developed science.[28] Part of the additional complexity of Sidgwick's position arose from the fact that, while he wished to promote the authority of specialists, he partly understood himself as a

---

[27] HS, 'The pursuit of culture as an ideal', *Miscellaneous Essays*, 359, 354. Cf. his comments in the debate on abolishing Greek as a compulsory entrance requirement at Cambridge, denying that he wished that science students could have more time to devote 'to their special studies': 'I entirely agree with those who deprecate any such specialisation' (*Mem*, 511).

[28] Émile Durkheim, 'L'individualisme et les intellectuels', *Revue Blanche*, 10 (2 July 1898), 7–13; see the discussion in Fritz Ringer, *Fields of Knowledge: French Academic Culture in Comparative Perspective 1890–1920* (Cambridge: Cambridge University Press/Paris: Editions de la Maison des Sciences de l'Homme, 1992), 223–5, and 304–6 for Durkheim's generalisation of the case for specialisation in his *De la division du travail social*.

specialist in the coordination of other specialisms. The university was to be recognised as the chief source of licensed expertise without losing the prestige of also being the home of 'culture'.

3. *Cultural authority and public debate*

The questions I want to focus on in the remainder of this essay concern the ways in which, drawing on these conceptions of what it was to be both a philosopher and a professor, Sidgwick contributed to public debate in the 1880s and, especially, the 1890s. Since his role here involved exercising a kind of cultural authority, it may help to begin by considering his own understanding of the form such authority needed to take at the end of the nineteenth century. In a paper he read to the Synthetic Society in 1899, Sidgwick noted 'that men are more and more disposed only to accept authority of a particular kind', namely 'the authority of a scientific "consensus of experts"'. He contrasted this with what he called 'theological authority':

> That is, it is not the unconstrained agreement of individual thinkers, pursuing truth with unfettered independence of judgement and unfettered mutual criticism, encouraged to probe and test the validity of received doctrines as uncompromisingly and severely as their reason may prompt, and to declare any conclusion they may form with the utmost openness and unreserve.[29]

One of the striking things about this passage is that it proceeds entirely by means of an extended negative: in characterising what theological authority is *not*, his chosen terms are themselves all negatives— 'unconstrained', 'unfettered', 'uncompromisingly', 'unreserve' and so on. It is interesting to see that in writing to Wilfrid Ward in advance of the meeting at which these claims were to be discussed, Sidgwick explained that 'my paper is likely to turn on the profound difference

---

[29] HS, 'Authority, scientific and theological', paper read to the Synthetic Society 24 Feb. 1899; printed as Appendix 2 in *Mem*, quotation at 609–10. Sidgwick had in fact been adumbrating a broadly similar view of authority since at least his *Ethics of Conformity and Subscription* of 1870; see Schultz, *Essays*, 41–2.

between modern scientific authority and theological authority, the for-mer being the unconstrained consensus of unfettered enquirers after truth, and the latter being—but the adjective here requires careful thinking over'.[30] As so often with Sidgwick's careful thinking, we never do quite arrive at a single adjective; hence the sequence of negatives.

The belief that there was an increasing number of issues on which the unconstrained judgement of experts converged was clearly impor-tant to Sidgwick's fragile sense of optimism, but in the present context it raises two questions. First, in so far as an issue was one on which experts could speak *as* experts, did this suggest that it was a matter where it would be at least wilful and perhaps irrational to disagree? And secondly, were philosophers to be regarded as 'experts' in this sense, and if so, what were they experts *about*? As I shall suggest, one effect of this emphasis on expertise may have been precisely to *remove* certain topics from public debate, an outcome which Sidgwick may actually have been keen to encourage.

I shall explore these questions by considering some of the arenas in which Sidgwick chose to try to exercise his authority in this period, and this will lead us into some of the more neglected aspects of his late writ-ings. The first of these arenas was constituted by the various Ethical Soci-eties which he contributed to or presided over. It is worth remarking that the largest single category of essays from this final period of Sidgwick's career began as addresses to various Ethical Societies (six of which are published in *Practical Ethics*, plus a further one in *Miscellaneous Essays*). These societies were mostly founded in the late 1880s, partly taking their inspiration from the Ethical Culture movement in the United States, and they represented an unstable coalition of earnest seekers after some source of moral light other than that traditionally offered by Christianity.[31] Looking at them historically, we would now have to say that these societies, especially the London Ethical Society at which Sidgwick spoke most often, also tended to have an implicit political agenda, which focused attention on individual moral improvement rather than on

[30] HS to Wilfrid Ward, 16 Jan. 1899; *Mem*, 572.
[31] See Ian MacKillop, *The British Ethical Societies* (Cambridge: Cambridge University Press, 1986); Gustav Spiller, *The Ethical Movement in Great Britain: A Documentary History* (London: Farleigh Press, n.d. [1934]).

collectivist measures of social reform (the idealist philosopher Bernard Bosanquet, who with his wife was one of the pillars of the staunchly individualist Charity Organisation Society, was the leading light of the London Society). The short-lived London School of Ethics and Social Philosophy (to which Sidgwick delivered two of his late ethical addresses) had been set up as, in effect, the teaching arm of the Ethical Society, but also perhaps as something of a counter to the Fabian-inspired London School of Economics established two years earlier.[32]

In addressing these societies, therefore, Sidgwick was only reaching a limited and self-selecting public, partly populated by fellow academic philosophers, albeit largely idealists, and partly by that stratum of educated men and women who flocked to the Settlements and similar benevolent institutions in London in the 1880s and 1890s, earnestly desiring to do good to their fellow man, especially to that man who was paid barely a living wage but who still drank too much. For the most part, in addressing such groups, Sidgwick did not attempt to pursue ethical first principles, but to assume the existence of a good will which was perhaps in need of the offices of a philosopher if it was to be clarified and made coherent.

In these addresses, he explicitly raised the question of whether the task of 'moral construction' should not be carried out entirely 'by experts, ... in short, by philosophers'. He admitted that he had initially sympathised with this idea, but that he had come round to believing that 'the work undertaken cannot be thoroughly well done by philosophers alone', partly because they lacked a sufficient range of information, and partly because their moral judgement needed to be 'aided, checked, and controlled by the moral judgement of persons with less philosophy but more special experience'.[33] There is potentially an interesting question here of who is helping whom in the enterprise of 'moral construction'.

---

[32] It folded within three years, but its successor was eventually absorbed into the LSE's Department of Social Work. See Ralf Dahrendorf, *A History of the London School of Economics and Political Science 1895–1995* (Oxford: Oxford University Press, 1995), 95; J. H. Muirhead, *Reflections of a Journeyman in Philosophy* (London: Allen and Unwin, 1940), 89.

[33] HS, *Practical Ethics: A Collection of Addresses and Essays* (London: Swan Sonnenschein, 1898), 31–4.

We may explore the implicit sense of role involved by looking in some detail at one of these addresses, entitled 'The morality of strife', delivered to the London Ethical Society in 1890. After the usual Sidgwickian preliminaries (which, as usual, take up more than half the essay)—the drawing of careful distinctions, the setting aside of topics which may appear to form part of the subject-matter but which on closer inspection do not really do so, the mention of issues which would require more careful scrutiny on another occasion, and so on—we come, finally, to the question of attempting to avert or restrict strife, including thereunder both war between states and conflict between groups or classes within a state. Sidgwick was, of course, not optimistic about the chances of averting warfare altogether, though he thought that on the issue of partially humanising its conduct, the nineteenth century had some reason to feel pleased with itself. As far as averting or reducing conflict was concerned, he believed that only strictly limited success was to be hoped for from what he called 'the external method', namely that of arbitration by an independent tribunal or other third party. The task for morality above all, therefore, was to try 'to reduce its causes by cultivating a spirit of justice'. Here humanity's report-card did not make such happy reading: 'There is hardly any plain duty of great importance in which civilised men fail so palpably as in this.' Still, Sidgwick maintained that people could be brought to perform this judicial function considerably better 'if national consciences could be roused to feel the nobility, and grapple practically and persistently with the difficulties of the task'. Certainly 'the thoughtful and moral part of every community' might do this better (did a slight *frisson* of self-recognition ripple through his audience at this point?).

He went on to urge that in the period before a conflict actually breaks out, 'it is surely the imperative duty of all moral persons, according to their gifts and leisure, to make an earnest and systematic attempt to form an impartial view of the points at issue'. He spelled out how this involved attempting to see things from the other side's point of view and so on, and he regretfully acknowledged that it is 'hard to bring a man to this when once the complex collision of principles and interests has begun, and it is still harder to bring a nation to it; but it is a plain duty imposed on us by reason' (the Sidgwickian universe seemed to contain an uncommonly high number of 'plain duties'). The same considerations, he insisted, apply to conflict within a state such as that between opposed class interests. Again, the method of external arbitration is likely to have only limited success:

> The only sure way of preventing strife within modern states from grow-ing continually more bitter and dangerous lies in persuading the citizens, of all classes and sections, that it is not enough to desire justice sin-cerely; it is needful that they fit themselves, by laborious and sustained efforts to understand the truths mingled with opposing errors, for the high and deeply responsible function, which democracy throws on them, of determining and realizing social justice so far as it depends on government.[34]

In best Sidgwickian fashion, I want to leave aside the many interesting questions which might be raised about this essay, and instead concen-trate on what might be termed a grammatical or syntactical version of Lenin's famously pithy question: 'Who whom?' In the passages I have cited, there are several verbs whose subjects are not specified, and my interest lies in trying to tease out who these subjects might be assumed to be. Who, for example, is to 'rouse national consciences'? Who are the 'thoughtful and moral persons', especially those with considerable 'gifts and leisure', who should 'attempt to form an impartial view'? Who is it who has the hard task of 'bringing people' to this perspective, even trying to 'bring the nation' to it? Who is the 'we' upon whom reason has imposed this 'plain duty'? And who, finally, is to 'persuade' the citizens of a modern democracy of the strenuous efforts they, as citizens, are obliged to make to establish what justice requires? These phrases all seem to assume the existence of, to adapt a phrase, a tightly knit group of ethically motivated men; they seem to advocate, in another idiom, a kind of moral vanguardism, as though the most strenuous requirements of morality were only freely to be spoken of among consenting adults in the privacy of Conway Hall. This was cer-tainly the preferred scale of the 'public' at which Sidgwick aimed.

---

[34] HS, 'The morality of strife', first published in *The International Journal of Ethics* in 1890, and reprinted in *Practical Ethics*, 105–8, 111–12. An ambiguity in the 'Preface' may have led the detail of its prior publication to be omitted: v–vi, cf. 83.

One of the many duties Sidgwick did undertake with exceptional scrupulousness, as we know from the successive editions of his major books, especially *The Methods of Ethics*, was that of revising and updating his published views. Comparison of the version of this essay as it appears in *Practical Ethics* in 1898 with that first published eight years earlier in *The International Journal of Ethics* shows how seriously he took this task, even in the case of his most occasional writings. The numerous changes are mostly not of great significance for my argument here, but they do suggest how sensitive to circumstances he intended his ethical strenuousness to be. Thus, by 1898 'the burning question of strife between industrial classes' required several pages where it had been passed over in a phrase in 1890. Similarly, in 1898 he added a section to counter the case put by 'some thoughtful persons seriously concerned for moral excellence who would regret the extinction of war', which may just have been a response to the increasingly bellicose, 'manly' temper of imperialist Britain in the 1890s, but which may more specifically have been provoked by the celebrated recent statements of this case by figures like Oliver Wendell Holmes Jnr and William James.[35] In addition, the sense of obligation appears to be strengthened in several places. Thus, where in 1890 he had merely offered a bland observation about the duty of states to resist 'unscrupulous aggression', in 1898 he added the more strenuous requirement that 'the duty is no less clear for any individual in the aggressing country to use any moral and intellectual influence he may possess—facing unpopularity—to prevent the immoral act'. In similar vein, perhaps, when discussing the duties of 'the thoughtful and moral part of every community' in the event of war, he in 1898 simply omitted a phrase which in 1890 had allowed that 'when the struggle has commenced, it is doubtless right for most if not all men to side with their country unreservedly'. And what had in 1890 been simply a 'duty of all moral persons ... to form an impartial view' had in 1898 hardened into an 'imperative duty'. And that narrowing of aim that Sidgwick would have called realism is also in evidence: for instance, where in 1890 citizens

---

[35] See particularly Holmes's 1895 Harvard address on 'A soldier's faith', in Max Lerner (ed.), *The Mind and Faith of Justice Holmes* (Boston, Mass.: Beacon, 1943).

had the 'high and deeply responsible function' thrown on them by democracy of 'deciding and declaring social justice', this had shrunk by 1898 to that of 'determining and realizing social justice so far as it depends on government'—the task has been framed in slightly more practical terms and seems to call for rather less mere 'declaring'. Re-publication in book form, especially in Sonnenschein's 'Ethical Library', implied reaching a slightly broader, or at least less definitely specifiable, audience, but the strenuous requirements being laid upon the moral élite are certainly not being relaxed.[36]

A somewhat different aspect of the role which Sidgwick wanted the philosopher to play in a certain kind of public debate is illustrated by another address from this collection, entitled 'The pursuit of culture', first delivered in 1897. His starting-point here was that 'culture' had by this date become a widely accepted ideal, appealed to even as the goal of social reform where that would enable the working class to cultivate their mental capacities and so on. He presented his own task here as being, characteristically, 'to free this fundamental notion, so far as possible, from obscurity and ambiguity'. And, he seems slyly to suggest, if obscurity and ambiguity are what is at issue, then who better to turn to than Matthew Arnold? He then spends some time teasing out the different senses of 'culture' to be found in Arnold's various writings, before distilling the relevant sense in the following terms:

> It is the love of knowledge, the ardour of scientific curiosity, driving us continually to absorb new facts and ideas, to make them our own and fit them into the living and growing system of our thought; and the trained faculty of doing this, the alert and supple intelligence exercised and continually developed in doing this,—it is in these that culture essentially lies.

While it is true that some of this hits the authentic Arnoldian note—especially the 'love' of knowledge and the 'alert and supple intelligence'—one cannot help remarking the presence of some rather

---

[36] Compare the essay as printed in *The International Journal of Ethics*, 2, 5, 6, 14, with the version in *Practical Ethics*, 87, 89–90, 93, 106. Note his sardonic reference to the problem of dealing with issues 'in a manner that would satisfy or edify the "plain man" for whom my little volume was supposed to be written'; HS to Mandell Creighton, 30 Aug. 1898; *Mem*, 569.

unArnoldian elements, such as the emphasis on 'scientific' curiosity, or on the importance of 'new facts', and above all the idea that one's thought must form a 'system', albeit one that is 'living and growing'. Not surprisingly, having built these elements into his definition of culture, Sidgwick concludes that Arnold cannot show us how this capacity is to be acquired, for Arnold's 'method of seeking truth is a survival from a pre-scientific age. He is a man of letters pure and simple; and often seems quite serenely unconscious of the intellectual limitations of his type.' (Here Sidgwick risks sounding disconcertingly like Arnold's *faux-naïf* self-mocking of his own 'want of principles systematic and interdependent' and so on; one almost expects Arminius to be appealed to as the authority on the latest advances of science in Prussia.) It is interesting to see that, scarcely a decade after Arnold's death, Sidgwick can so confidently dismiss his approach as irretrievably out of date. 'Intellectual culture, at the end of the nineteenth century, must include as its most essential element a scientific habit of mind; and a scientific habit of mind can only be acquired by the methodical study of some part of what the human race has come scientifically to know.'[37] 'Culture' was supposed to be the man of letters' trump card, but 'intellectual culture' is here promoted as the outcome of 'methodical study', clearly a strenuous activity not likely to be successfully pursued in Grub Street.

Having established that art, science, and morality are by no means identical to each other, he attributes to Arnold the claim that 'it is the special function of literature to comprehend and mediate between these divergent aims and views'. But the task, Sidgwick rules, is beyond literature's powers.

> For to satisfy completely the demand to which he appeals, to bring into true and clear intellectual relation the notions and methods of studies so diverse as positive science and the theory of the fine arts is more than

[37] HS, 'The pursuit of culture', *Practical Ethics*, 220–22, 223. This essay clearly overlaps in many places with that published first in pamphlet form as *The Pursuit of Culture as an Ideal*, and subsequently in edited form in *Miscellaneous Essays*. The first was given as an address to the London School of Ethics and Social Philosophy, the second to the students of the University College of Wales, Aberystwyth, both in the autumn of 1897.

> literature as literature can perform; the result can only be attained by
> philosophy, whose peculiar task indeed it is to bring into clear, orderly
> harmonious relations the fundamental notions and methods of all special
> sciences and studies.

Literature, 'though it cannot give philosophic form and order', 'may
give a provisional substitute for philosophy to the many who do not
philosophize'. It can help to produce a harmony of feeling in our con-
templation of the world, 'if not the reasoned harmony of ideas which
only philosophy could impart', something that would seem to be
beyond the grasp of 'the many who do not philosophize'. And as for the
fundamental question as to whether science and morality conflict, 'This
is a difficulty with which only a systematic moral philosophy can deal.'[38]

One cannot help noticing that in each of the last three passages I have
quoted, the phrase 'only philosophy' recurs. The public task of putting
the pursuit of culture on a sound footing, he suggests, can only be properly undertaken by philosophers, although there is the suggestion of a
variant on his 'two-tier' view I mentioned earlier, as though philosophy
is for the few and literature for the many. Sidgwick was thus attempting
to see off the cultural hegemony of the man of letters, just as in his better-
known essays he attempted to see off the challenge of the sociologists
and evolutionary naturalists more generally.[39] For all their modesty of
tone, these essays suggest a job-description for the position of cultural
arbiter which severely narrows the field of potential applicants.

4. *Royal Commissions*

I want now to turn to the other major semi-public forum in which
Sidgwick acted with some frequency in the 1890s, namely the highly
distinctive one of the Royal Commission. Sidgwick sat on or was

---

[38] *Practical Ethics*, 227, 228, 230.
[39] Cf. Turner's conclusion: 'Sidgwick did not claim a dominant position for the
philosopher in contemporary culture, but he did demand recognition of the intellectual
inadequacy of men of science as sole arbiters of English thought'; Frank M. Turner,
*Between Science and Religion: A Reaction to Scientific Naturalism in Late-Victorian
England* (New Haven: Yale University Press, 1974), 65.

invited to give evidence to no fewer than four such commissions in the course of the decade, revealing along the way his strong sense of the possibility of deploying intellectual authority and expertise to help determine policy. The first was the Royal Commission on New Statutes for the Proposed Gresham University in London: Sidgwick was one of thirteen members of the Commission, under the chairmanship of Earl Cowper, which took evidence from May 1892 to May 1893, and published its report early in 1894 (its recommendations were largely incorporated in the act establishing the University of London in 1900).[40] Sidgwick threw himself into the work of the Commission at a time when he was overburdened with other labours, leading to one of his periods of overwork—his sense of duty in such matters was acute. This was perhaps all the more true given his awareness as the Commission proceeded that, as he wrote to his wife, 'so much labour is thrown away, e.g. all the labour I am spending on the New University, as far as I can see'.[41] This presumably referred to the fact that Sidgwick was, vainly as it turned out, opposing the principle of uniting in one institution the dual functions of being an ordinary teaching university based in London and giving degrees through external examinations to students across the country. He signed the final report but appended a dissenting note in which he argued this case, where he forcibly expressed his conviction that the reputation of a university was jeopardised if it was reduced to no more than an examining mechanism for students whom it had had no hand in forming.[42]

The Royal Commission on Secondary Education set up by Lord Rosebery's government in 1894 had as its chairman one of Sidgwick's oldest friends and fellow 'academic liberals' from the 1860s, James Bryce, and Eleanor Sidgwick was one of its three female members.[43]

---

[40] See H. Hale Bellot, *The University of London: A History* (London: Athlone, 1969), ch. 5.

[41] HS to his wife, Dec. 1892; *Mem*, 525.

[42] *Report of the Royal Commission on the New Statutes for the Proposed Gresham University in London* (1894), Cmd 7425; 'Note' by Sidgwick, lix–lx. For the work of the Commission, see also Negley Harte, *The University of London 1836–1986* (London: Athlone, 1986), 150–56.

[43] Ethel Sidgwick, *Mrs Henry Sidgwick*, 133–4.

Sidgwick was one of those from whom written answers were solicited to a series of questions bearing particularly on the relations between the universities and schools. In his reply, he acknowledged that at first the work of the local examinations syndicate (of which he was a member at Cambridge) may have been 'a little amateurish', but that in the last generation 'the range of university studies has continually extended', and so it could now act with the requisite professional authority even in new fields such as modern languages. He urged the universities to teach technological subjects and to make provision for vocational education, including the training of teachers, but his strongest plea was for the removal of compulsory Latin and Greek as an entry requirement at Cambridge—'no reform in our academic system is at present so urgently needed'—not least on account of the impact such a change would have in encouraging the 'modern side' in schools. His broader concern to make the scholarly authority of the university as widely effective as possible is evident throughout his answers.[44]

The other two commissions were both on economic, indeed fiscal, matters, and are an indication of Sidgwick's considerable reputation as a political economist, at least in official circles. In its final report, published in 1896, the Royal Commission on the Financial Relations Between Great Britain and Ireland included a long memorandum by Sir Robert Giffen, head of the statistical section of the Board of Trade, discussing the basis on which taxable property should be assessed in Ireland and in Britain. Sidgwick had been sent Giffen's memorandum by the Commission and asked to comment. His 'Note' is interesting, partly for its general argument against according Ireland any separate fiscal status, but partly because he at one point mildly challenged Giffen's appeal to 'economic authority', which Sidgwick then glossed as referring to 'English economists', of whom he clearly saw himself as one. Sidgwick's comments recognised Giffen's eminence as a statistician, but implied that he was weaker on the *principles* of

---

[44] *Report of the Royal Commission on Secondary Education* (1895), Cmd 7862, Vol. V: 'Memoranda and Answers to Questions'; Sidgwick's reply is at 243–7, quotation at 244, 246. See also H. A. L. Fisher, *James Bryce*, 2 vols (London: Macmillan, 1927), I, 295–9.

taxation, upon which there was an established body of theoretical work.[45]

When in 1897 the Conservative government was setting up a Royal Commission on Local Taxation, it would seem (from a letter to Arthur Balfour in the Balfour Papers) that Sidgwick was asked if he would be willing to serve on it.[46] In the event, Sidgwick did not become a member of the Commission itself, but he was none the less given the opportunity to submit his views directly to the Commissioners when a list of questions was sent out to sixteen 'financial and economic experts', mostly academics. Sidgwick sent an extremely long and detailed answer on the equity of the present system of local taxation, demonstrating his command both of the facts of existing arrangements and of the principles on which they could be justified.[47] The general tenor of his submission would not have been unwelcome to the Tory government of the day, most notably his statement: 'I conclude, therefore, that the principle on which partial relief from rates was granted to the owners of agricultural land in 1896 is sound from the point of view of equity.'[48] This, in the context of the politics of the 1890s, was a striking endorsement of what the authoritative history of the subject has described as 'the most controversial legislative measure of 1896', since

[45] *Final Report of the Royal Commission on the Financial Relations Between Great Britain and Ireland* (1896), Cmd 8262; 'Note on the Memorandum by Sir Robert Giffen' by Henry Sidgwick, 180–83, quotation at 183. Interestingly, when Sidgwick had given a paper on taxation at the Political Economy Club in London in 1886, Giffen was the one person he mentioned by name in his journal record of the occasion; *Mem*, 447.

[46] 'When you asked me, on Tuesday, if I should like to be on the new Commission, I answered the question simply; I should not like it. But if you asked me to undertake the work as a public duty, I should not think it right to refuse. To have a right to refuse I should require a much stronger conviction than I actually have of the value to mankind of my philosophic studies.' HS to A. J. Balfour, 16 Apr. 1897; Balfour Papers, BL Add Mss 49832, f. 91.

[47] Cf. the later comment of his Cambridge colleague Henry Jackson: 'I think he would have liked nothing better than to be Chancellor of the Exchequer', not perhaps a comment it is easy to imagine being made about many leading intellectual figures; *Mem*, 376.

[48] *Report of the Royal Commission on Local Taxation* (1899), Cmd 9528, 'Volume of Memoranda on Imperial and Local Taxes'; Answers by Henry Sidgwick, 99–112, quotation at 112.

it represented 'an unprecedented subsidy for the landed interest'.[49] Not perhaps for the first time in the 1890s, Sidgwick's scrupulously measured analysis issued in acceptance of some of the most blatantly ideological features of the *status quo*.

Royal Commissions were in some ways an ideal medium for Sidgwick: reasoned argument and a respect for the evidence seemed to stand a better chance of determining the outcomes than in the rough and tumble of public discussion in a democracy. Above all, they accorded a significant role to expertise. They functioned for Sidgwick as the best expression of that perennial ideal of the well-connected 'insider', the hope of shaping policy without having to engage in politics. If one wanted a formula to cover his activities in this sphere it might perhaps be the time-honoured one of 'helping the authorities with their enquiries'.

5. *National politics*

In so far as Sidgwick did have a public identity in national politics in this period, it was, at least after the Home Rule crisis of 1886, as a Liberal Unionist. He voted Liberal for the last time at the election of November 1885; by August 1886 he is describing himself as one of 'the altogether insignificant handful of Academic Unionist Liberals', and in December 1886 he went up to London to attend an initial meeting of the Liberal Unionist secession.[50] For some years thereafter, he figured in Liberal Unionist activities both nationally and locally.[51] In 1887 he

---

[49] Avner Offer, *Property and Politics 1870–1914: Landownership, Law, Ideology, and Urban Development in England* (Cambridge: Cambridge University Press, 1981), 207–8. The 1896 Act effectively reduced the rateable value of agricultural land to compensate for the loss of revenue caused by the decline in agricultural rents.

[50] *Mem*, 430; 453; 462.

[51] The inaugural dinner of the Liberal Unionist Club took place on 30 March 1887, with the Marquess of Hartington presiding, at which their organ, *The Liberal Unionist*, was launched. Sidgwick's close friend A. V. Dicey was among those who spoke, and afterwards Dicey recorded his private opinion that the Unionists 'represent the best moral feeling' in the country (Richard A. Cosgrove, *The Rule of Law: Albert Venn Dicey, Victorian Jurist* [London: Macmillan, 1980], 141). Sidgwick was for a while active

'headed the Liberal Unionist deputation to Lord Hartington from the universities', and signed the 'memorial' to Hartington published in *The Times* on 27 June 1887.[52] The question of Home Rule continued to stir Sidgwick's political feelings, especially what he saw as the 'disgrace' of the unprincipled abandonment of Irish landowners envisaged in Gladstone's later proposals.[53] It is intriguing that as late as 1898 maintaining the distinct identity of Liberal Unionism should still matter so much to him: in that year he mentions being a member of the Liberal Unionist council and being at a meeting with 'the Duke' (that is, of Devonshire, as Hartington had become on his father's death), though he could be ironic about the pitfalls of the Liberal Unionists 'pos[ing] as a specially intelligent part of the community'.[54] By then they represented no more than a principled rump, but all along Liberal Unionism had been a classic political example of the problem of being all chiefs and not enough Indians, though for Sidgwick, with his increasing hostility to the noisiness of popular politics, this may actually have been part of its appeal.

Sidgwick's chief compassion-in-arms among Liberal Unionists at Cambridge was J. R. Seeley, a friend with whom he shared close intellectual as well as political sympathies.[55] One important facet of Sidgwick's identity which the connection with Seeley brings out is the common Comtean link between a belief in the growth of scientific

among Cambridge Liberal Unionists: in February 1888, for example, he was one of the leading local figures hosting a big Liberal Unionist meeting in Cambridge at which Dicey spoke (Robert S. Rait [ed.], *Memorials of Albert Venn Dicey* [London: Macmillan, 1925], 127).

[52] *The Times*, 27 June 1887, 6; for the academic Liberal Unionists, see Christopher Harvie, *The Lights of Liberalism: University Liberals and the Challenge of Democracy 1860–86* (London: Allen Lane, 1976), 226, 228–9.

[53] *Mem*, 523, on his reasons for voting Conservative in the 1892 election.

[54] HS to Lady Rayleigh, 10 Feb. 1898; *Mem*, 555. On the absorption, for all practical purposes, of the Liberal Unionists in the Tory Party in the course of the 1890s, see Peter Marsh, *Lord Salisbury and the Discipline of Popular Government: Lord Salisbury's Domestic Statecraft 1881–1902* (Hassocks: Harvester, 1978).

[55] For Seeley's prominence among Liberal Unionists, see Deborah Wormell, *Sir John Seeley and the Uses of History* (Cambridge: Cambridge University Press, 1980), 169–73.

authority and a disdain for popular politics, indeed any politics. Seeley, a more unbridled Comtist (a more unbridled everything), genuinely believed that 'political differences would disappear in the light of science';[56] meanwhile, he had little but scorn for the 'anarchy' of party politics and the 'talking shop' that was Parliament. His academic commitment to developing a 'science of politics', a project which Sidgwick supported and, in his more cautious fashion, also tried to promote, was partly animated by a larger conviction about the movement from the 'metaphysical' to the 'positive' stage in human history.[57] By the 1890s, Sidwick's own Comtism was decidedly vestigial, but for both men, I suspect, Liberal Unionism, in being opposed to the 'demagoguery' and 'sentimentalism' of current politics, appealed as the best interim expression of a more scientific approach to political questions.

As suggested earlier, Sidgwick's position on domestic policy tended to be markedly conservative in the 1880s and 1890s. He served for four years as acting chairman of the Cambridge branch of the Charity Organisation Society, and he tended to follow the COS line in opposing all 'relaxations' of the Poor Law system; he was even critical of Arthur Balfour's speech introducing the Medical Relief Bill of 1885 (which removed the disqualification from voting for those who received medical relief only) as likely to undermine 'the movement towards providence which all true philanthropists who know the poor are doing their utmost to support'.[58] But the politics of the 1890s were increasingly dominated by foreign and colonial issues, and here Sidgwick displayed an interesting mixture of liberal principle and conservative caution. He sympathised with the agitation against the 'Armenian atrocities' of 1896, but, revealingly, he now looked at such issues as though through Downing Street windows:

> I have not heard from A.J.B. anything of what is being done (I suppose it to be a Cabinet secret if there is anything) ... It seems to *me* that at the present stage it would be a mistake for England to try isolated action: but I am inclined to approve the agitation going on, as more likely to

---

[56] Wormell, *Seeley*, 172.
[57] See Collini, Winch, and Burrow, *That Noble Science*, esp. 225–34. Sidgwick edited Seeley's posthumous *Introduction to Political Science* (London: Macmillan, 1896).
[58] *Mem*, 506; HS, journal entry 19 July 1885; *Mem*, 417–18.

strengthen the hands of the Government than to weaken them—at least so long as it is kept on the present lines.[59]

This is surely 'Government House Utilitarianism' with a vengeance.[60]

His response to the Boer War was perhaps more revealing still. In private, Sidgwick expressed strong disapproval of the British government's policy that led to the war. For example, he wrote to Bryce in November 1899: 'As for the war, I do not mind telling you privately that no political event in my lifetime has ever been so odious to me. It seems to me the worst business England has been in since the war with the American colonies, and I cannot help foreboding that it will end similarly, in an independent Dutch republic.'[61] And in February 1900, he wrote to another friend: 'I thought the war unjustifiable on any principle of International right, and on the whole indefensible on grounds of policy, though I admit the situation a difficult one.'[62] Some of his correspondents shared his views, though it is clear that his larger circle of acquaintances mostly did not. At the end of 1899 he apologised to one correspondent for not having written for a long time, 'but I have been for some months in the exceptional position—among my friends—of disliking and disapproving of this war and foreboding that it will end in disgrace and disaster to England'. He avoided some of the most delicate difficulties of his position by concluding that if any one figure was culpable it was Milner even more than Chamberlain.[63]

Sidgwick's personal ties with the government were very close by this point. He frequently stayed with his brother-in-law, Arthur Balfour, where he met other leading Tory figures including Salisbury (and he clearly enjoyed being, as he had put it earlier, 'at the centre of information').[64] One cannot help remarking that on the evening before Sidgwick was to be operated on for the cancer which killed him soon

[59] HS to H. G. Dakyns, 15 Sept. 1896; *Mem*, 549.
[60] I take the phrase 'Government House Utilitarianism' from Bernard Williams's criticism of Sidgwick in *Ethics and the Limits of Philosophy* (London: Fontana, 1985), 108–9.
[61] HS to James Bryce, 6 Nov. 1899; Bodleian Library Oxford, Bryce Papers, 15, f. 99.
[62] HS to H. G. Dakyns, 3 Feb. 1900; *Mem*, 580.
[63] HS to Lord Tennyson, 25 Dec. 1899; *Mem*, 576–8.
[64] HS, journal entry 18 June 1885; *Mem*, 412.

thereafter, he and his wife dined alone with Balfour and his sister 'in the large dining-room at 10 Downing Street'.[65] But more than personal loyalty underlay his habitual perspective. In *The Methods of Ethics* he had, perhaps a little incautiously (if that adverb can ever be applied to him), used the phrase 'from the point of view ... of the universe', with which Bernard Williams had memorable sport in his criticism of utilitarianism.[66] But it is fair to say that in the last decade of his life, at least, Sidgwick thought that the proper perspective from which to approach political issues *was* 'from the point of view of the government'. As I have suggested elsewhere, it is surely revealing that he could implicitly equate the analysis of 'the chief general considerations that enter into the rational discussion of political questions in modern states' with the attempt 'to treat systematically the chief questions for which the statesman has to find answers'.[67]

The consequences of this disposition were most tellingly illustrated when his friend and fellow philosopher, James Sully, wrote to him soliciting his support for making some kind of public statement against the war. At first Sidgwick responded by saying, at least as recorded by Sully, that he would like 'to help in preserving the independence of this brave people', but (striking a more characteristic note) that 'he thought it, however, most undesirable to publish anything of the sort at that crisis'.[68] In March 1900 he then wrote to Sully to explain why he had decided against signing the petition for stopping the war which Sully was helping to organise. 'Perhaps it is partly my personal connection with the Government', he explained somewhat defensively, 'which makes me think, in considering a question of this kind, "What should I do if I were the Government?"' Putting that question to himself at the present juncture, he concluded that it would not be right simply to halt the war without obtaining certain securities and safeguards for the

---

[65] *Mem*, 589–90.

[66] Bernard Williams, 'The point of view of the universe: Sidgwick and the ambitions of ethics', *Cambridge Review*, 7 (1982); partly repeated in *Ethics and the Limits of Philosophy*, 107–9.

[67] Collini, 'Ordinary experience', 358–9, quoting *Elements of Politics*, 6, and *Philosophy*, 26.

[68] James Sully, *My Life and Friends* (London: Fisher Unwin, 1918), 286.

future (about, for example, the rights of non-Boers in South Africa). 'I should think this my duty, taking up the matter at this stage, in spite of my strong condemnation of the diplomacy that brought the war about.' But he recognised that he could not find any measure which would thus bring the war to an honourable end as circumstances stood at present. 'This is why I decided not to sign.'[69]

In considering the question of roles, it is pertinent to observe that not all Sidgwick's academic colleagues felt obliged to be similarly judicious: several were more outspoken on either side. In Cambridge, Westlake, the Whewell Professor of International Law, delivered a public lecture essentially justifying the war, while other senior members such as Oscar Browning and A. C. Pigou spoke against it at the Union and elsewhere.[70] That it was possible to be both a prominent philosopher and a leading academic figure *and* still to be outspoken in opposition to the war is indicated by the example of Edward Caird. The keeper of the flame of British Idealism had been Master of Balliol for six years when the Boer War began, but that did not stop him expressing the strongest support for its critics. The journalist W. T. Stead was one of the leading anti-war agitators, and Caird wrote to him in September 1899, 'cordially sympathising' with his efforts and emphatically declaring that 'such a war would [be] both a crime and a blunder'.[71] Once the war had actually begun he 'showed where his sympathies lay by taking the chair for Miss Hobhouse on one occasion when she visited Oxford in connection with her efforts on behalf of the Boer women and children in the concentration camps', a very unpopular cause at the time.[72] Nor was it impossible to be a Liberal Unionist and a critic of the war, though it was naturally rarer than among those who had remained

---

[69] HS to James Sully, 29 March 1900; *Mem*, 581–2.

[70] Westlake's *The Transvaal War* was given as a lecture in Cambridge on 9 Nov. 1899, and reviewed in the *Cambridge Review* (23.11.99), 102–3; for Browning and Pigou see Stuart Wallace, *War and the Image of Germany: British Academics 1914–1918* (Edinburgh: John Donald, 1988), 13–14.

[71] As reported in *The Manchester Guardian*, 28 Sept. 1899; reproduced in Stephen Koss (ed.), *The Pro-Boers: The Anatomy of an Antiwar Movement* (Chicago: University of Chicago Press, 1973), 23.

[72] Henry Jones and J. H. Muirhead, *The Life and Philosophy of Edward Caird* (Glasgow: Maclehose, 1921), 153.

within the Liberal fold; Leonard Courtney, for example, was a prominent Liberal Unionist of widely admired high principles who became
one of the most consistent (and most vilified) spokesmen for the 'Pro-
Boer' position.[73]

One way to try to get a clearer sense of Sidgwick's 'roles' in comparative perspective may be to ask whether one could imagine him
signing an English equivalent of 'le manifeste des intellectuels' in
protest against the government's handling of an English Dreyfus Affair.
That question may seem to assume too many improbable counterfactual conditions, but one can well imagine Sidgwick being wary of
the medium of expression as well as of the outspoken content; certainly
he was the last person we can imagine being seduced by the glamour
of dissidence. By this stage his preferred course of action would more
probably have been to murmur in Arthur Balfour's ear that the government's position might be considered in some quarters to be somewhat
injudicious.

6. *Roles and duties*

The first edition of the *Oxford English Dictionary*, the relevant volume
of which was compiled some years after Sidgwick's death, treats 'role'
as a French word, always circumflexed, usually italicised, and suggests
that even when used figuratively it still alludes to its theatrical origins:
to 'play' a role is to play a part or character, to be 'in the *rôle* of x'.
There are few more improbable incarnations in which we could imagine Sidgwick than got up in costume and greasepaint, strutting before
the footlights, the handsome *jeune premier* declaiming his lines to a
packed house (and of all the incongruities here, not the least may be the
juxtaposition of Sidgwick and the idea of 'a packed house'). Still, I
think that the tension between social performance and inner identity
which the language of 'roles' always suggests may be helpful when
considering Sidgwick's later career. It seems to me possible that he at

[73] See Koss, *The Pro-Boers*, 29–31, 266–7; also L. T. Hobhouse and J. L. Hammond,
Lord Hobhouse: A Memoir (London: Arnold, 1905).

times felt that his roles imposed duties whose performance he found merely dutiful. This had fairly obviously been true of his crisis over subscription to the Thirty-nine Articles in 1869; as he put it in the pamphlet which he issued on that occasion: 'There is no danger to religion which an earnest person more deplores and dreads than that there should insinuate itself into his religious exercises a sense of their shadowiness and unreality; a feeling that the view of the universe which they are framed to suit is not precisely that which his innermost self actually takes.'[74] But he perhaps came to feel something similar about his professorial 'exercises' on more than one occasion. 'A professor must write books', but it is an interesting question how far Sidgwick felt it a positive obligation as a professor to write such dull books.[75] Metaphors about letting oneself off the leash may suggest something which in Sidgwick's case seems inappropriately canine, but I wonder whether in his journal and his more intimate letters we do not catch glimpses of a certain straining against the constrictions of public judiciousness, and if so, whether this might not have contributed to what I am diagnosing as a certain ambivalence about participating in public debate.

This may perhaps make a small contribution to the resolution of the major question which no honest reader of Sidgwick can avoid, namely, how was it that this exceptionally clever and, by all accounts, delightful man managed, in some of his later writings, to be so heart-sinkingly boring? Anyone who has read at all extensively in Sidgwick's writings from both the 1860s and the 1890s is bound, I think, to feel mildly depressed at what happened to his prose. The best pieces from the earlier period show him excelling in the arts of the polemical essayist— consider his witheringly cogent critique of the reality of a classical education, or the deft, stylish criticism of Matthew Arnold on culture, or the imaginative sympathy and delicacy of phrasing in the essay on

---

[74] HS, *The Ethics of Conformity and Subscription* (London: Williams and Norgate, 1870), 27.

[75] 'Still man must work—and a Professor must write books'; HS to J. A. Symonds, 1 Dec. 1887; *Mem*, 481. Or again: 'Decidedly nature intended me to read books and not to write them; I wish the former function was regarded as a sufficient fulfilment of Professorial duty'; HS, journal entry 15 Dec. 1886: *Mem*, 463.

Clough. And although the prose of *The Methods of Ethics* is naturally
more analytical and impersonal, still the argumentative subtlety and the
sheer, sustained architectonic command displayed across that long
book make it far from boring. But by the 1890s, these qualities can
sometimes seem to have been replaced by little more than a ponderous
judiciousness. There are still certain themes which can stir faint echoes
of his better literary self: he can still write with some attack and conviction about the higher education of women, and in combating a current intellectual fad like sociology he is driven to some crisp arguments
and telling phrases. But far more often, especially when writing (as he
most frequently did in this period) on some large general issue in ethics
or politics, his prose constructs a kind of airless chamber in which all
interesting questions wilt and die.

This seems to me most obviously true of his heavy treatises of the
period, *The Principles of Political Economy* and *The Elements of
Politics*,[76] and it was clearly something of which Sidgwick was aware
(consider his reflection after reading the reviews of the former work
that the defect he would *not* be able to remove in revising it would be
'the one damning defect of long-winded and difficult dulness'[77]—a
comment which would have the virtue of being endearing did it not
possess so much of the prior virtue of being true). But it is revealingly
true of *Practical Ethics* also—revealing because he is not in this latter
case constrained by the requirements of system and comprehensiveness
imposed by a treatise, and also because several of the topics discussed
touched quite closely on his own personal dilemmas. But time after
time, as we move through the first half or even two thirds of one of
these essays in which he elaborately clarifies terms and sets boundaries,
what had at first seemed like a rich and absorbing topic gets shrivelled
into a thin, dry question to which, once precisely formulated, the
answer is more or less obvious.

Some of this may, sadly, be put down to age as Sidgwick's
naturally cautious temperament drove his mind along ever more

---

[76] See the discussion of the latter in Collini, 'Ordinary experience', and esp. Sidgwick's
confession (in the letter to Bryce quoted at 345–6) of the 'barrenness' of some of his
analysis.

[77] HS, journal entry 8 Jan. 1885; *Mem*, 397–8.

deeply etched grooves; some of it may be put down to his sheltered life, his relatively restricted, and largely complacent, social circle, leading him to treat what was purely contingent in social arrangements as given. But somewhere along the way, I blame philosophy— or, to be a bit less provocative, the way Sidgwick applied his conception of philosophy as 'reflective analysis' to non-philosophical subjects. Philosophy proceeds, remember, by 'the method of reflection on the thought we all share, by the aid of the symbolism we all share, language'. And earlier, in *The Methods of Ethics*, he had said of 'common-sense morality', to the analysis of which he devotes such a large part of that book, that it is to be taken 'quite empirically, as we find it in the common thought expressed in the common language of mankind'.[78] But the danger of this method when applied to practical issues may be precisely to assume that there is more consensus in the 'common thought' of mankind than is really the case, and it may be partly for this reason that he tends to regard 'controversy' as the result of misunderstanding or lack of clarity, rather than genuine disagreement. After all, what becomes of the philosopher's role in public discussion of those matters on which 'we' do not 'all' share the same 'thought'? Sidgwick, I have been arguing, oscillates between largely withdrawing from public debate and only entering it in tutelary mode in order to reduce it and perhaps even to bring it to an end. Temperament and circumstances obviously played a part in this, but so, too, I am now suggesting, did his conception of the contribution philosophical analysis could make. If professors of philosophy were properly fulfilling their role and its duties, as Sidgwick appears to conceive them, then it would be hardly surprising if the effect were to reduce, even perhaps to come close to eliminating, public debate, as more or less all 'controversy' was shown to be 'unnecessary'. This seems to me to help explain why it is that Sidgwick often appears to come upon contemporary lay discussion like a schoolmaster coming upon a collection of small boys playing a rowdy, disorganised game of football: he explains that he is uniquely trained to act as referee, and he then methodically proceeds to demonstrate that most of their attacking

---

[78] HS, *The Methods of Ethics* (1874), 7th edn (London: Macmillan, 1907), 229.

moves are misguided, to reduce the size of the goals to near invisibility, and to entirely deflate the ball.

Others may be better qualified than I am to pursue the analysis of similarities between this conception of the role of philosophy and that found in the so-called 'Oxford philosophy' or 'linguistic analysis' of the late 1940s and 1950s.[79] The impact on academic philosophy itself was very different in the two cases, partly no doubt because Sidgwick did not gather about him a school on the scale that Ryle and Austin did; in terms of shaping the discourse of professional philosophy in Britain as a whole, size was almost everything. But there may have been some functional resemblance in the broader cultural role involved: both idioms tended to have the effect of lowering the temperature of all discussion to the point where one is left with little more than a small pile of freeze-dried particulars. Sidgwick was certainly not guilty of either the coercive dismissiveness or the schoolboy jokiness displayed by 'Oxford philosophy' at its worst, but the absence of these characteristics, though no doubt admirable in itself, hardly made his prose livelier.

Sidgwick's later career, I have been suggesting, does not quite correspond to any of the major models offered by recent historiography: this is most evident, perhaps, in the case of the French 'intellectuel', though his distance from the model of the German 'mandarin' will also by now be clear. But in this phase of his life he also stands at some remove from the classic 'public moralist' of the high-Victorian period. Here we need to recall the various publics that Sidgwick addressed and the media through which he reached them. It is noticeable, I think, how often in this period he is to be found speaking to some relatively small learned body or intellectual society of some kind—the Political Economy Club, Section F of the British Association, various Ethical Societies, the Synthetic Society, the Eranus, university philosophical clubs and so on. These might be seen as in some ways the cultural equivalents of Royal Commissions,

---

[79] Cf. Jonathan Rée, 'English philosophy in the fifties', *Radical Philosophy*, 65 (Autumn 1993), 3–21. It is interesting to consider how far Rée's strictures on the 'method of linguistic analysis' (p. 17) might apply to Sidgwick's 'method of reflective analysis'.

select bodies guaranteeing a level of informed discussion. It is certainly striking that during this period Sidgwick published virtually nothing in newspapers, a few letters about purely academic business aside, and practically nothing for the political weeklies; furthermore, he wrote hardly anything for the monthly magazines and only a handful of pieces for the great quarterlies. His periodical publication was now confined to *Mind* and *The International Journal of Ethics* above all, plus some contributions to the house journals of particular organisations such as *The Classical Review* or the journal of the Charity Organisation Society. And, turning to a medium which some of the high-Victorian public moralists had made notable use of, he delivered no genuinely public speeches, and of course he declined all suggestions that he might stand for Parliament. In other words, Sidgwick entered into genuinely 'public' debate in the 1880s and 1890s only to a very limited extent. In so far as he did so, his prime aim was the elimination of 'unnecessary controversy' and the combating of 'dangerous' notions, where 'dangerous' meant, as he put it in 1894, 'liable to fill the mind of the confiding reader with a vain illusion of knowledge'.[80] In some respects, the force of much of Sidgwick's later writing may be seen as tending to *reduce* the cultural authority of the individual public moralist, especially of the kind that was exercised through exhortation, tone, literary personality, and so on, and as tending to replace it with the authority of collective, impersonal knowledge.

But nor is he an uncomplicated example of Heyck's thesis about the formation in the latter part of the century of a self-consciously separate intellectual class marked by withdrawal from the public domain, specialisation of intellectual focus, and professionalisation of career.[81] He may in some ways appear to have been a standard-bearer for what is called, in an ugly translation of the prevailing French term, 'the autonomisation of the university field'. But even here one has to recognise his place among wider political and literary élites: after all,

---

[80] For 'unnecessary controversy', see Collini, 'Ordinary experience', 341; HS, 'Political prophecy and sociology' (1894) *Miscellaneous Essays*, 219.
[81] See Heyck, *Transformation of Intellectual Life*, 224–6.

his main ally in the early stages of the scheme that eventually became the British Academy was James Bryce, hardly the model of the 'pure' academic. In European terms, Sidgwick perhaps corresponded more to the older figure of the 'notable', a personage who was of consequence in the community partly through social connection, partly through institutional role, and partly by virtue of personal gifts or capacities. In English terms, he may have been an early example of a type which became more familiar by the mid-twentieth century: the socially well-connected don, one who made a career by attaining eminence in a branch of scholarship, but one whose social experience gave him both the confidence and means of access to contribute directly and indirectly to the policy-making process, largely by-passing general public debate.

What I am pointing to, therefore, are certain structural parallels or symmetries among Sidgwick's conceptions of his various roles. As a philosopher, he entertained both an intellectually imperial and a more practically restricted sense of the reach of his subject; as a professor, he combined a fairly austere notion of the propriety of concentrating on the scientific advance of one's discipline with a capacious sense of the need to make the authority of the university tell in society; and as a participant in the public arena, he displayed a marked ambivalence, on some occasions feeling the obligation to take up the polemical cudgels against various forms of half-truth, but more frequently wishing rather to limit than to stimulate public debate, preferring to act within carefully selected groups or even behind closed doors.

These roles, and the tensions generated by the relationship between them, were not, of course, unique to Sidgwick, even though the detail and the shading reflect his particular career and temperament. He should, rather, be seen as belonging to the first generation in Britain in which the possibility presented itself of being a fully professional academic who also played a public role. Since then, many academics, needless to say, have confined themselves to cultivating their specialist gardens, just as, conversely, many public commentators have not aspired to make a mark in a scholarly discipline. It is the peculiar burden of the academic intellectual to have to live with the tension which comes from moving *between* these roles, never wholly at rest at either pole, never wholly at ease with the movement between them. On this score, perhaps none of us can do other than respect the efforts of this 'sinful man who partly tried to do his duty'.[82]

[82] Sidgwick left instructions that if no church service were to be used, he would like the following words to be said over his grave: 'Let us commend to the love of God with silent prayer the soul of a sinful man who partly tried to do his duty. It is by his wish that I say over his grave these words and no more.' *Mem*, 599.

Ethics, Utilitarianism, and Positive Boredom

JONATHAN RÉE

A MORAL PHILOSOPHER who has the distinction of dying in 1900 is liable to bear a heavy burden of retrospective wisdom about nineteenth-century moralism in general. And Henry Sidgwick is in any case well qualified to serve as an exemplar. He was one of the chief mourners at God's long Victorian funeral, and he conducted himself, on the whole, with the kind of laboriously agonised seriousness which most of us, I suspect, find enviably impressive and touchingly ludicrous at the same time. As an old-fashioned moralist, Sidgwick comes true to type.

Stefan Collini has expressed well-founded doubts about the idea that the dynamics of Sidgwick's intellectual milieu were governed by a single uniform process of 'professionalisation'.[1] He voiced them some years ago in *Public Moralists*, and he has now elaborated the point with the very helpful suggestion that Sidgwick's sense of professional duty is better explained in terms of the several different 'roles' he found himself playing on the Victorian intellectual scene: as 'philosopher' and 'professor' principally, and to some extent as 'public moralist' as well. Each of these roles, Collini argues, entailed different duties, and their mutual interference was responsible for Sidgwick's complicated if not contradictory attitudes to the new forms of academic life, from his reservations about specialisation within the university (p. 21) to his

[1] Stefan Collini, *Public Moralists: Political Thought and Intellectual Life in Britain, 1850–1930* (Oxford: Oxford University Press, 1991), 199–205.

Proceedings of the British Academy, **109**, 51–57. © The British Academy 2001.

concerns for the authority of the 'academic person' outside it (p. 21). These preoccupations, Collini thinks, together with Sidgwick's activities in various Ethical Societies, in the Charity Organisation Society and in the movement for higher education for women, refuse to fit in with any simple idea of professionalisation.

But in one way Collini seems to have grown closer to the professionalisation hypothesis over the years. There was just one place in *Public Moralists* where he alluded to the fact that Sidgwick 'was not a thrilling speaker',[2] but he now listens out for his drone with all the attentiveness of a parent listening for an infant's crying. He suggests, indeed, that in the twenty years leading up to his death at the age of 62 Sidgwick became 'so heart-sinkingly boring' (p. 43) that one has to wonder whether he 'felt it a positive obligation as a professor to write such dull books' (p. 43).

I have not spent as much time as Collini tuning in to Sidgwick's longueurs, but I venture to suspect that he has not quite got the measure of them. For one thing, Sidgwick was not an exceptionally boring writer, at least by the prevailing standards of British philosophy; and it is worth remembering that he was noted for a habit of sprinkling his speech—which was often impeded by a stammer—with a characteristic kind of verbal frivolity which came to be known as 'Sidgwickedness'.[3] For another, it is important to distinguish between different varieties of literary boringness. Some prose is boring because it imparts its information very slowly and with no detectable expressive pulse: it is boring because of a lack of skill and self-discipline on the part of the author. But there is also prose which is boring because it has been deliberately drained of affect, as if for fear that the smallest breach in the wall of impassivity would soon lead to its total collapse and an overwhelming flood of embarrassing emotion. Such boringness—positive as opposed to negative—is the result of too much self-discipline rather than too little, and if Sidgwick was boring, it was more in the positive than in the negative style.

[2] Collini, *Public Moralists*, 200.
[3] I have this information from a conversation with Mrs Anne Baer, daughter of a nephew of Henry Sidgwick, at the British Academy conference on Sidgwick on 18 March 2000.

Collini analyses Sidgwick's professionalism, including his professional boringness, mainly in terms of his roles as professor and philosopher. But as far as Sidgwick himself was concerned, the relevant *dramatis personae* were slightly different, as he showed in an essay of 1899 where he presented himself at one point 'as a Professor of ethics', and at another, 'as a utilitarian'.[4] If he was subject to a conflict of roles, it may be that it depended on the difference between ethics, in the traditional and elevated sense of the word which he had perhaps once given his heart to, and the bathetic utilitarianism which is recognised as its modern nemesis.

Towards the end of his life, Sidgwick wrote an autobiographical sketch about how he became the person who would write *The Methods of Ethics* in 1874. As an undergraduate at Trinity College Cambridge in the 1850s, he explained, he had been trained in moral philosophy on the basis of the textbook *Elements of Morality* by the Master of his College, the overweening William Whewell. Whewell had been elected to the Knightbridge professorship at Cambridge in 1838, and immediately changed the title of the Chair from 'Moral Theology or Casuistry' to 'Moral Philosophy' and transformed the seventeenth-century sinecure into a serious educational responsibility. The professorship became a platform, if not a pulpit, for the propagation of 'Moral Truths', and Whewell undertook to formulate them 'in a definite and permanent manner' and to demonstrate that they were 'rationally connected with each other' so as to form a 'system of Independent Morality'.[5]

But Whewell's conscientious work as Professor of Moral Philosophy, and also as pioneer of the 'Moral Sciences' course, first examined in 1851, did not always have the effect he aimed at. Sidgwick recalled that the main thing he had learned from Whewell's teaching was that 'Intuitional moralists [such as Whewell] were hopelessly loose', which made him realise that the 'moral rules' he had been 'educated to obey' might be 'doubtful and confused' or indeed 'dogmatic, unreasoned,

---

[4] HS, 'The relation of ethics to sociology', *International Journal of Ethics* (1899), reprinted in *Miscellaneous Essays and Addresses* (London: Macmillan, 1904), 249–69; see 256, 266.
[5] See William Whewell, *Lectures on Systematic Morality* (London: John W. Parker, 1846), 2, 20.

incoherent'. It was then that he encountered John Stuart Mill's utilitarianism, which gave him 'relief' for a while. But then he realised that Mill was unable to fend off the threat of egoism, in other words the habit of valuing one's own interest, however slight, more highly than the most vital interests of everyone else. 'No doubt it was, from the point of view of the universe, reasonable to prefer the greater good to the lesser,' Sidgwick wrote, but 'it seemed to me also undeniably reasonable for the individual to prefer his own.' (Collini reminds us that Sidgwick's reference to 'the point of view of the universe' has been mocked by a more recent Knightbridge professor, but in this context the phrase is used somewhat ironically to describe a position which Sidgwick was not sure he had the right to assume, rather than one he could arrogate to himself without qualms.)

After Mill, Sidgwick turned to Kant, but Kant too proved unable to defeat egoism. Sidgwick came to feel, as he said, like 'a disciple on the loose', in desperate need of 'sympathy and support', if not indeed of a 'master'.[6]

So it was very curious that Sidgwick should have ended up writing a book which would serve as a text for the Moral Sciences programme at Cambridge, and stranger still that he should himself take over the Knightbridge Chair of Moral Philosophy in 1883. Collini attributes the intensification of Sidgwick's boringness partly to this professorship, but he also assigns it to another source: 'somewhere along the way,' he says (p. 45), 'I blame philosophy.' In particular he blames the slyly self-denying ordinance by which philosophers have cast themselves as 'under-labourers' engaged in nothing more substantial than 'reflective analysis' of ideas devised by others, and he quotes Sidgwick's gloomy comment, in 1887, about having 'philosophised himself into a conviction of the unprofitableness of philosophy' (p. 18).

Sidgwick's doubts about philosophy are, as Collini notes, somewhat similar to those which led to a new epidemic of philosophical dullness with the rise of linguistic analysis some sixty years later. But in fact they were much less sweeping and far more subtle, for if

---

[6] This account was included in the Preface to the posthumous sixth edition of *The Methods of Ethics* (London: Macmillan, 1901), xvii–xxiii; see xvii, xviii.

Sidgwick was disappointed by philosophy's past achievements, he still entertained hopes for its future. He noted that philosophy was 'still—after so many centuries—in a rudimentary condition as compared with the more special studies of the branches of systematised knowledge that we call Sciences', but he thought that the correct response would be activism rather than despair. Whilst admitting that 'no one can hope to remove suddenly and quickly so ancient and inveterate a deficiency', he affirmed that 'it ought to be the aim of all earnest students of Philosophy to remedy this defect'.[7]

That at least was Sidgwick's assessment of 'Theoretical Philosophy'. But when he came to 'Practical Philosophy' he was less sanguine, and—contrary to what Collini seems to imply—he can hardly have imagined that he would be able to repair the defect by adopting 'Common Sense' as his master. Collini points out that Sidgwick criticised his colleague James Stuart, MP for Hackney, for pronouncing on political issues without first examining the 'accepted theories and systematic methods of reasoning' concerning them; but he is wrong to suggest that Sidgwick thought such theories and methods deserved unconditional respect. He simply thought they were matters which 'an educated person ought at any rate to show adequate knowledge of, even if he intends to banish them to Jupiter or Saturn' (p. 21).

Sidgwick's treatment of 'the Morality of Common Sense' in Book III of *The Methods of Ethics* is also less complacent than Collini suggests. He reproaches him for assuming 'that there is more consensus in the "common thought" of mankind than is really the case' (p. 45) and implies that Sidgwick always interpreted clashes of opinion as if they were simply the effects of 'misunderstanding or lack of clarity'. And after noting that Sidgwick defined philosophy in terms of 'the Dialectical Method', meaning 'the method of reflection on the thought which we all share, by the aid of the symbolism which we all share, language', he asks rhetorically what Sidgwick could do if it turned out that '"we" do not "all" share the same "thought"?'[8] (p. 13).

---

[7] HS, *Philosophy, its Scope and Relations*, published posthumously (London: Macmillan, 1902), 13.
[8] *Philosophy*, 49.

But Sidgwick was not assuming that we all think the same thoughts, any more than that we all speak the same language. He made it clear in his autobiographical sketch that Book III of *The Methods of Ethics* had been written in conscious imitation of Aristotle, whose discussion of the moral virtues was, he thought, no more than an idealised transcription of 'the Common Sense Morality of Greece'. The task he set himself in Book III, he explained, was simply 'to do the same for *our* morality here and now'.

The upshot was not an unthinking endorsement of common-sense morality, but on the contrary an access of 'fresh force and vividness' for Sidgwick's perception that common sense was full of 'doubtfulness and uncertainty'. He had managed, with a certain amount of hermeneutic bullying, to show that the morality of common sense pointed in the same general direction as utilitarianism, but he knew that it also contained the elements of the loose dogmatism which, as a young man, he had found repellent in Whewell. And even if it now approximated to the two great principles to which he now subscribed, namely Kant's version of the golden rule (that 'whatever is right for me must be right for all persons in similar circumstances') and Mill's version of utilitarianism (that we 'should act in such a way as to promote universal happiness'), it did not always and necessarily do so. When confronted with better arguments, according to Sidgwick, common sense would always have to yield.[9]

The real and excruciating difficulty for Sidgwick was that he did not think that decisive arguments about the fundamental methods of ethics would ever be found. Even if common sense tended to converge on utilitarian conclusions, egoism still remained a theoretically viable option. The three methods—egoism, intuitionism and utilitarianism—thus constituted 'alternatives between which ... the human mind seems to me necessarily forced to choose'.[10] Practical philosophy here reached its *ne plus ultra*, and the one certainty about the foundations of ethics was that they would always be uncertain.

Collini recounts a shocking story about the young Alfred Marshall

---

[9] See *Methods*, 343, n. 1, and Preface to sixth edition, xxi–xxii.
[10] *Methods*, 12.

reproaching Sidgwick for failing to inspire his students with moral fervour in the manner of T. H. Green. It was an extraordinary impertinence, but Sidgwick was large enough to regard it as 'interesting', noting that the reason for his comparative failure was simply that he thought there were no grounds for the kind of passionate conviction that made Green's lectures legendary: 'the deepest truth I have to tell', as he wrote in his journal, 'is by no means "good tidings"'. If that made him boring, he could not help it, for beneath his unyielding exterior he still suffered from the wounds of his discovery that the 'Moral Truths' propounded by Whewell were groundless, and of his subsequent realisation that the virtues prized by the various moralities of common sense do not always exactly coincide with the prescriptions of utilitarian calculation. If he was cold, it was not from a lack of inward passion. Rather like John Stuart Mill, he kept himself under severe control for fear of being overwhelmed by intellectual grief.

In an early essay on J. R. Seeley's *Ecce Homo*, Sidgwick had affirmed the need for 'magnanimity' in place of the 'resentment' that so often characterised Christianity,[11] and over the years he certainly managed to make himself magnanimous. He had no patience with the exquisite theatricality of Matthew Arnold's sadness, but he would surely not have resented having to share the distinction of dying in 1900 with another great moral philosopher, equally exasperating and no less anguished, who had also been shattered by his contact with utilitarianism. Sidgwick would surely have found it 'interesting' that Friedrich Nietzsche acknowledged the extraordinary achievements of 'utilitarian Englishmen' in their special field of endeavour, which of course was none other than 'boringness'. The English utilitarians should be encouraged, Nietzsche explained, because 'to the extent that they are boring, their utility can hardly be exaggerated'.[12] Nietzsche died on 25 August, Sidgwick three days later—both of them escaping at last from the terrible violence wrought by their philosophical intelligence on the consoling platitudes of morality.

[11] HS, '*Ecce Homo*' (1866), in *Miscellaneous Essays and Addresses*, 1–39; see 33.
[12] Friedrich Nietzsche, *Zur Genealogie der Moral* (1887), Vorrede §4, in *Kritische Studienausgabe*, edited by Giorgio Colli and Mazzino Montinari, Vol. 5, 250–51 and *Jenseits von Gut und Böse*, §228, ibid., 165.

SECTION II

Three Methods and a Dualism

JOHN SKORUPSKI

SIDGWICK DISTINGUISHES three methods of ethics: intuitionism, egoism and impartialism (as I shall call it).[1] Yet he holds that just two of these, egoism and impartialism, are grounded in 'practical reason'—and in fact he famously concludes that these two methods constitute an irreducible 'dualism of the practical reason'.

We still remain, I think, uncertain of the relations between morality, self-interest, and an impartial theory of the good. And the persistence, integrity and penetration of Sidgwick's ethical thought give his conclusions as to these relations a continuing authority. However, they also raise questions in a usefully clear way. Notably: if there are three methods, why should there be only a *dualism* of practical reason? Or,

---

[1] Sidgwick calls it the method of utilitarianism—which he also calls 'universalistic hedonism'. However, the contrast that is of interest here (and which interested Sidgwick) is between the egoistic thesis that the good of any individual has an agent-relative rational claim on that individual's deliberation—together with the method(s) founded upon that view—and the impartial thesis that the good of any individual has an agent-neutral claim on anyone's deliberation, together with the method(s) founded on *that* view. For this purpose we do not need to decide on the truth or otherwise of hedonism, but neither do we need to decide on the specific distributive doctrines of aggregative or average utilitarianism. Impartialism as such says only that the good of any individual is agent-neutrally good, that is, that any individual has reason to promote it. Aggregative or average utilitarianism makes further assumptions about the form of the function from individuals' goods to the agent-neutral good, and there are many other plausible options. But the choice between them is not relevant here. See John Skorupski, *Ethical Explorations* (Oxford and New York: Oxford University Press, 1999), chs 3 and 5.

Proceedings of the British Academy, **109**, 61–81. © The British Academy 2001.

otherwise put, if the method of intuitionism is not grounded in practical reason, what establishes, of either of the other two, that *it* is? My conclusions will be anti-Sidgwickian. I shall argue that if 'practical reason' is construed broadly it is characterised by a wide diversity of irreducibly warranted—though not indefeasible—practical dictates or principles, of which prudence is one. On the other hand if practical reason is construed narrowly, conceived one might say as *pure* practical reason, then it exhibits a characteristic unity: so conceived, its sole warranted and indefeasible principle is a principle of impartiality in assessment of the good. Either way practical reason is not dual. These conclusions, as I say, are anti-Sidgwickian; I hope none the less that what follows can be accepted as a homage to Sidgwick.

1. *Intuition and reason*

The method of the intuitionist is that of investigating common-sense morality to identify its dictates in general or particular cases. Sidgwick calls these dictates 'intuitions', by which he means '"immediate judgement[s] as to what ought to be done or aimed at"'.[2] They are 'immediate', he explains, in that they appear as *knowledge* in their own right and not as knowledge derived from something else. And he notes that any method of ethics must ultimately rest on at least one such 'intuition'—on a judgement as to what ought be done or aimed at which appears as evident in its own right; and which is, on that basis, regarded as 'immediately known to be true'.[3]

So when Sidgwick calls something an intuition he means that it appears as knowledge in its own right. He does not mean that it *is* knowledge. He makes this explicit later, when he notes that the term 'intuition'

> has sometimes been understood to imply that the judgement or apparent perception so designated is *true*. I wish therefore to say expressly, that by calling any affirmation as to the rightness or wrongness of actions

[2] HS, *The Methods of Ethics*, 6th edn (London: Macmillan, 1901), 97.
[3] In that sense, he notes, the egoistic and universalistic methods are also 'intuitional'.

'intuitive,' I do not mean to prejudge the question as to its ultimate validity, when philosophically considered: I only mean that its truth is
apparently known immediately, and not as the result of reasoning. I
admit the possibility that any such 'intuition' may turn out to have an
element of error ... indeed the sequel will show that I hold this to be to
an important extent the case with moral intuitions commonly so-called.[4]

What distinguishes the intuitionist is thus not just the claim that
common-sense morality contains a large diversity of such intuitions,
but the further claim that these intuitions, or at least some of them or
some part of them, are authentic, underived bits of knowledge.

Does Sidgwick simply disagree with this claim? For a writer who
makes such efforts at precision, I find it extraordinarily hard to be sure.
One possible interpretation would say that he does. On this interpretation Sidgwick thinks that no principle of ordinary morality is *immediately known* to be true; such principles, or rather their more precise
correlates, can only be *known* by being derived from the utilitarian
principle which is itself immediately known. Thus the method of the
intuitionist[5] founders because it finds no genuine intuitive knowledge.
On this interpretation it is not puzzling that Sidgwick thinks that there
is only a dualism of practical reason even though there are three
methods of ethics. For one of these methods turns out to yield no
normative knowledge in its own right.

However, on another possible interpretation Sidgwick does not
deny that common-sense morality contains some intuitive knowledge.
On this interpretation, Sidgwick is prepared to accept that common
moral intuition does yield some underived or immediate *knowledge* of
normative truths, insisting only that its knowledge is unclear and
imprecise—and indeed that it also contains an 'element of error'. On
this interpretation his claim is only that the knowledge it does yield
cannot be made 'scientific'—clear and precise—by the method of the
intuitionist alone. Thus in the last paragraph of his 'Review of Common
Sense' (*Methods*, Book III, ch. xi) Sidgwick says:

---

[4] *Methods*, 211.
[5] The 'dogmatic intuitionist': ibid., 102. For discussion of how Sidgwick understands
the term 'intuition', and of when intuition yields knowledge, I am indebted to Robert
Shaver.

> Nothing that I have said even tends to show that we have not distinct moral
> impulses, claiming authority over all others, and prescribing or forbid-
> ding kinds of conduct as to which there is a rough general agreement, at
> least among educated persons of the same age and country. It is only
> maintained that the objects of these impulses do not admit of being sci-
> entifically determined by any reflective analysis of common sense. ... the
> Morality of Common Sense may still be perfectly adequate to give prac-
> tical guidance to common people in common circumstances: but the
> attempt to elevate it into a system of Intuitional Ethics brings its inevitable
> imperfections into prominence without helping us to remove them.[6]

Here Sidgwick does not, it is true, explicitly say that these 'distinct
moral impulses' amount to intuitive knowledge—only that they are
'perfectly adequate to give practical guidance'. But in what sense
'adequate'? The most obvious reading is that they yield adequate
knowledge for practical purposes. For Sidgwick's only point against
them is that their objects cannot be 'scientifically determined'—made
precise—by reflective common sense alone. And it is obvious that there
can be knowledge that is not *precise* knowledge, so unless Sidgwick
has surprisingly overlooked this point he could perfectly well grant that
common-sense morality yields such knowledge, which is adequate for
(most) practical purposes.

Consider how he deals with a particular such moral impulse, that of
gratitude:

> the duty of requiting benefits seems to be recognized wherever morality
> extends; and Intuitionists have justly pointed to this recognition as an
> instance of a universal intuition. Still, though the general force of the
> obligation is *not open to doubt (except of a sweeping and abstract kind
> with which we have not here to deal)* its nature and extent are by no
> means equally clear.[7]

He proceeds to highlight the unclarities. But pointing out such unclarities is perfectly consistent with accepting that I know the following: (a)
that if a person has done me a lot of good out of sheer good will, I have
reason to be grateful and show it; (b) that lack of gratitude, taken far

---

[6] *Methods*, 360–61.
[7] Ibid., 259–60, my emphasis. I take it that the sweeping and abstract kind of doubt
could also be raised about my knowledge that there is a desk in front of me.

enough, can become blameworthy. The unclarity, or rather imprecision, of (a) and (b) is evident, but so is their truth. Would Sidgwick, if challenged, deny that we '*immediately*' know that truth? On the second interpretation, he would not. On this interpretation Sidgwick's view is that common-sense morality contains intuitive knowledge, though through lack of precision it cannot qualify as 'scientific' or 'philosophical' knowledge.[8]

In which case, why does Sidgwick think there is only a dualism of practical reason? Why doesn't the intuitive knowledge found by the intuitionistic method also count as part of practical reason? Is Sidgwick just identifying—indeed confusing—rationality with clarity and precision? Why should purely *rational* intuitions have to be clear and precise in a way that (a) and (b) are not? It would require substantive philosophical argument to establish that. Anyone who merely assumes it evinces a preconception about practical reason which could fairly be called rationalistic or scientistic.

I have just used the phrase 'purely rational intuition'. And this raises a variety of further questions. Is there a difference between an intuition and a purely rational intuition? What are we to understand by practical reason anyway? Further, if there is a plausible account of practical reason, or as I shall suggest later, *pure* practical reason, on

---

[8] Bk III, ch. xi sets up four criteria for 'moral axioms' (see §2, ibid., 338–43). They should (1) be stated in 'clear and precise terms', (2) be 'really self-evident', (3) not conflict 'with any other truth', and (4) be supported by an 'adequate "consensus of experts"'. He claims that no ordinary moral principles can satisfy (1). But his own list seems to allow that they could fail (1) and satisfy (2)–(4)—in particular, they could be imprecise and yet still 'really self-evident'.

Further, in his chapter on 'The Relation of Utilitarianism to the Morality of Common Sense' (Bk IV, ch. iii) Sidgwick explicitly disclaims the hypothesis that 'the perception of the rightness of any kind of conduct has always—or even ordinarily—been derived by conscious inference from a perception of consequent advantages'. Ibid., 457. It is, he concedes, 'not as the mode of regulating conduct with which mankind began, but rather as that to which we can now see that human development has been always tending, as the adult and not the germinal form of Morality, that Utilitarianism may most reasonably claim the acceptance of Common Sense'. Ibid., 457. This raises very interesting questions about the connections between morality's epistemology and its history. And it's at least compatible with the (second interpretation) view that the 'intuitions' of common-sense morality have an immediate or underived default warrant, and at least in some circumstances constitute knowledge.

which the immediate intuitions of common-sense morality don't belong to pure practical reason, what epistemic status do they have and in particular how do they constitute knowledge?

We shall not be able to address the last of these questions at all fully. However, I shall argue that a distinction between 'intuition' and 'purely rational intuition' is not pointless. Many ordinary moral judgements are warranted in their own right without being derived, directly or indirectly, from any other more basic normative principle; in an important sense however they are not judgements of pure practical reason. The judgement that someone has acted in a blameworthily ungrateful way would be one example. On the second interpretation Sidgwick could agree with this. Contrary to Sidgwick, however, I shall argue that the egoist's principle must also be seen, epistemologically, in much the same way as these ordinary moral 'intuitions': like them, it is derived from nothing more basic—but like them, it is not a principle of pure practical reason either.

Distinct and irreducible sources of practical reasons, I shall suggest, underlie *each* of Sidgwick's three methods. But only the impartialist's principle, the principle that the good or well-being of any being is, simply, good, has its source in *pure* practical reason. In contrast (I shall argue), neither the reason-giving force of prudence nor that of morality is reducible to pure practical reason. In both cases it derives instead from the hermeneutics of the sentiments: in the case of morality, the sentiment of blame; in the case of prudence, that of desire.

To make this clear we shall have to distinguish carefully two separate questions. The first concerns the epistemic pedigree of a practical principle. Here the question is, from what source does the principle derive its (default) warrant? The second concerns its potential defeaters. The question in this case is whether the principle can be defeated by different principles stemming from another source.[9]

---

[9] I have shifted here from the concept of knowledge to that of warrant. Note that (i) a belief may be warranted but not true; (ii) a warranted belief may cease to be warranted in an improved state of information. The question Sidgwick raises about common moral intuition is whether it delivers any immediate knowledge. It could also be asked whether common moral intuition delivers any immediately warranted beliefs. I return to these questions in sections 5 and 6.

But before moving to these claims we must consider a perplexing question: how to *formulate* the alleged dualism of practical reason.

2. *The dualism of practical reason*

The preface to the posthumous sixth edition of *The Methods of Ethics* prints a manuscript draft in which Sidgwick gives a brief account of the development of his ethical view.[10]

Beginning, he writes, from an adherence to Mill's utilitarianism, he came to worry that it did not deal adequately with the conflict between self-interest and duty. He reread Kant and was impressed by Kant's fundamental principle, which he formulated for himself as the principle 'That whatever is right for me must be right for all persons in similar circumstances'. This, he thought, was 'certainly fundamental, certainly true, and not without practical importance'.[11] But it did not meet the difficulty which had led him from Mill to Kant: 'it did not settle finally the subordination of Self-Interest to Duty'. For a rational egoist could accept it. As a *rational* egoist he would accept that when any person is faced with a choice between his own and the general happiness the right thing for that person to do is to choose his own. 'The rationality of self-regard', Sidgwick continues, 'seemed to me as undeniable as the rationality of self-sacrifice. I could not give up this conviction, though neither of my masters, neither Kant nor Mill, seemed willing to admit it: in different ways, each in his own way, they refused to admit it.'[12] Delving back further in the history of ethics, he found that Butler had affirmed the same duality of interest and duty: 'he recognised a "Dualism of the Governing Faculty"—or as I prefer to say "Dualism of the Practical Reason," since the "authority" on which Butler laid stress must present itself to my mind as the authority of reason, before I can admit it'.[13] The final step was provided by Aristotle. Sidgwick came to see the significance of

[10] *Methods*, xv–xxi.
[11] Ibid., xvii.
[12] Ibid., xviiii.
[13] Ibid., xix.

Aristotle's interrogation of common-sense morality and the need to do the same himself.

> But the result of this examination was to bring out with fresh force and vividness the difference between the maxims of Common Sense Morality (even the strongest and strictest, *e.g.* Veracity and Good Faith) and the intuitions which I had already attained, *i.e.* the Kantian Principle ... and the Fundamental Principle of Utilitarianism'.[14]

He became increasingly convinced that common-sense morality was a 'system of rules tending to the promotion of general happiness. ... the morality of common sense showed me no clear and self-evident principles except such as were perfectly consistent with Utilitarianism'.[15]

Two points are noteworthy. First, in this account Sidgwick does not state any definite principle of rational egoism.[16] He merely points out egoism's consistency with the Kantian principle, which he understands as a principle of universalisability. Second, the answer to the question with which we were concerned in section 1, the question of what his view of the standing of common-sense moral maxims is, remains unclear here too. He says that his investigation forcefully and vividly showed the difference between them and the Kantian and utilitarian principles. He also says that the only moral maxims which seemed clear and self-evident were such as were consistent with the utilitarian—or in our terms, impartial—principle. Is he then accepting that some principles of the morality of common sense *are* clear and self-evident? On this reading (the second interpretation) ordinary morality contains principles which are self-evident in their own right—but they turn out on examination not to conflict with the impartial principle, whereas egoism and impartialism, also separately self-evident, do appear to conflict (unless we assume a moral government of the

---

[14] *Methods*, xx.

[15] Ibid., xxi.

[16] Indeed he never provides a suitable formulation of the egoist principle. Most of his formulations are statements of the irrationality of pure time-preference in decisions concerning one's own good—to that extent they are not clearly at odds with the impartialist's principle at all. Jerome B. Schneewind, *Sidgwick's Ethics and Victorian Moral Philosophy* (Oxford: Clarendon Press, 1977), chs 10 and 13, provides a valuable survey and discussion of Sidgwick's various formulations of his principles or axioms.

universe to reconcile them). And this then explains why Sidgwick is concerned with that particular dualism.

Clearly Sidgwick does not regard the dualism as an outright contradiction. For his point is that the two principles may come into conflict in the absence of a moral government of the universe. So the principles of egoism and impartialism should not be formulated in such a way as to be inconsistent outright. How then should they be formulated?

One might first of all consider the following:

(i)   The degree to which there is reason for me to do an action is proportional to the degree to which it promotes the good of beings overall, taking the good of all beings into account by some impartial principle.[17]

(ii) The degree to which there is reason for me to do an action is proportional to the degree to which it promotes my good.

These are not inconsistent, because it's possible, if unlikely, that there is always a perfect correlation between the degree to which an action promotes general good and the degree to which it promotes my good. However, these statements are too weak in that they don't specify what it is that *gives* me reason to perform an action. The impartialist's thought is not just a thought about a positive correlation which happens to hold between the strength of one's reason to do something and the degree to which doing it promotes general good. His claim, rather, is that only the fact that an action will promote general good to some degree *gives* one reason to do that action—and it gives it to *that* degree. Likewise, the egoist's thought is that only the fact that an agent's action will promote that agent's good to some degree *gives* the agent reason to perform that action—and it gives it to that degree.

But put like this, the thoughts of the impartialist and the egoist are directly contradictory. So perhaps we should we weaken them. We should say that the promotion of general good constitutes *a* reason for action and the promotion of one's own good also constitutes *a* reason for action. Thus:

---

[17] The last clause leaves open the question of what impartial distributive principle should be adopted.

(I)   The fact that an action will promote to some degree the good
      of beings overall, taking the good of all beings into account by
      some impartial principle, gives anyone a reason of propor-
      tionate degree to do that action.

(E)   The fact that an action will promote the agent's own good to
      some degree gives that agent a reason of proportionate degree
      to perform that action.

Yet this must now be weaker than what Sidgwick had in mind. For if
all we are saying is that (I) and (E) are both true, then it's unclear why
they should come into conflict at all, and in particular, unclear why a
moral government of the universe should be required to avert chaos. (I)
and (E) simply specify a type of fact which is reason-giving and further
specify the way in which that type of fact determines the strength of
that specific type of reason.

Indeed something like (E) straightforwardly follows from (I): holding effects on other people's well-being constant, the degree to which
an agent has reason to do an action varies proportionately with the
degree to which that action promotes the agent's good. For the agent's
own good is a constituent of general good. What was intended, however, was that (E) is somehow *independently* reason-giving. How are
we to explain this intended independence? One way to do it is by giving
an account of how reasons from the impartial source and reasons from
the egoistic source combine. On this approach the good of the agent
must have some special extra weighting in the practical reasoning of
the agent.

Suppose we gave some such account. It's not clear that that would
capture Sidgwick's intention. For we would now have a unified account
of the principle of practical reason—a universalism with an agent-
relative bias. There would be no scope for Sidgwick's worries about his
dualism. Sidgwick, after all, says that 'Practical Reason' feels a 'vital
need'

> of proving or postulating [a] connexion of Virtue and self-interest, if it is
> to be made consistent with itself. For the negation of the connexion must
> force us to admit an ultimate and fundamental contradiction in our
> apparent intuitions of what is Reasonable in conduct; and from this

admission it would seem to follow that the apparently intuitive operation of the Practical Reason, manifested in these contradictory judgements, is after all illusory.[18]

Evidently he does not imagine that impartialism and egoism combine into a consolidated principle. In some way he sees them as *competing* perspectives on practical reason. There is a perspective on practical reason which is egoistic and another perspective which is impartial. He takes them to be equally authoritative or inescapable, a sort of permanently forced gestalt switch or bifocalism. But he also thinks that if no 'legitimately obtained conclusion or postulate as to the moral order of the world' can guarantee their coincidence, then 'the apparently intuitive operation of the Practical Reason ... is after all illusory': in 'a recognized conflict between self-interest and duty, practical reason, being divided against itself, would cease to be a motive on either side; the conflict would have to be decided between one or other of two groups of non-rational impulses'.[19]

3. *Supererogation*

I find this a more interesting view than universalism with an agent-relative bias. It captures the point that the egoist's and impartialist's respective claims to give an account of the basic principle of pure practical reason are *hegemonic*. Sidgwick is sensitive to that point (no doubt he is helped here by his interest in the history of moral philosophy). But on the other hand it's not easy to say how he positively sees the relation between the two principles. Perhaps he didn't really think this through. I myself cannot see how a dualism of practical reason of the kind Sidgwick envisages can be coherently formulated. Sidgwick thinks that egoism and impartialism are not a priori contradictory but can lead to contradiction in conjunction with some plausible-seeming a posteriori factual propositions. (i) and (ii) fit that picture, but as we've noted are too weak inasmuch as they don't state what *gives* one reason to act. On

[18] *Methods*, 506.
[19] Ibid.

the other hand, if (I) and (E) are so strengthened as to become hegemonic, they also become directly contradictory, irrespective of what 'moral order' there is in the world. However, I won't pursue the question[20] of how to formulate the dualism because I want to propose that there is no such dualism—though I also want to try to explain why there might seem to be.

Let me approach this claim by considering a case in which egoism and impartialism clearly collide. It is also a case of supererogation—and that too helps to highlight the questions we need to ask ourselves.

Fred is holed up in a defensive position with his fellow soldiers. He's fighting against an evil enemy whose victory would greatly damage the general good. Now a grenade is thrown in. Fred's got three options. His best chance of saving himself is to run away, his next best is to take evasive action by throwing himself to the ground. But he could also throw himself on to the grenade. This last action, he knows, would save the most people. For he knows that his comrades won't run away—they can see that they have an obligation to stay at the post and go on fighting, and they'll do that. But they won't throw themselves on the grenade either. So if he throws himself on it, stifling its impact, more soldiers will be saved and the chance of resisting the evil enemy will be greater. This, then, is the action that will most promote general good. Coming to this conclusion, he throws himself on the grenade.

The impartialist will endorse this reasoning. But he can of course agree that the right *moral* assessment is that Fred went beyond the call of duty. Fred and his comrades had an obligation not to run away; but they did not have an obligation to fall on the grenade. Our morality is

---

[20] For more on this question see David Phillips, 'Sidgwick, Dualism and Indeterminacy in Practical Reason', *History of Philosophy Quarterly*, 15 (1998), 57–78. Phillips suggests that Sidgwick may have held an 'indeterminacy view' according to which there is both a rational obligation to maximise one's own good and a rational obligation to maximise good impartially—except when those obligations conflict, in which case what one rationally ought to do is indeterminate. (Presumably in that case there is still a rational obligation with disjunctive content—to maximise one good or the other.) This strikes me as a philosophically unattractive position, in that it's hard to reconcile with supervenience, that is, the point that it's *in virtue* of the fact that an action maximises my good, or impartial good, that I ought to do it. Why should this supervenience lapse when my good and impartial good conflict?

not heroic; it gives some latitude to self-concern. It's also sensible, in that it would be silly to require everyone in this situation to throw themselves on the grenade. Nevertheless, according to the impartialist, if Fred had his facts right, then he was also right to think that there was more reason for him to stifle the grenade at the cost of his life than just to take evasive action. What Fred did was admirable, though not morally obligatory, and according to the impartialist it was admirable because Fred rightly saw that it *was* what there was most reason for him to do and had the courage and spirit of sacrifice to do it.

A universalist with an agent-relative bias might take a different view. If his agent-relative bias was strong enough, he could say that there was most reason for Fred to take evasive action. Neither this view nor the impartialist's view is more in line with morality, in so far as morality only says that Fred has an obligation not to run away. It certainly doesn't say that Fred has an obligation *not* to throw himself on the grenade. Only the pure egoist view, which says that Fred should run away, is inconsistent with morality.[21] As to the bifocal view, it says that what there is most reason for Fred to do depends on whether one is focusing impartially or egoistically. Or, if we take seriously Sidgwick's view, which I quoted above—that in 'a recognized conflict between self-interest and duty, practical reason, being divided against itself, would cease to be a motive on either side; the conflict would have to be decided between one or other of two groups of non-rational impulses'—it simply ceases to provide rational guidance.[22] One thing that Fred doesn't have most reason to do on this last account is what most of us would do—that is, fall to the ground.

Personally I find the impartialist account most plausible. Fred's courage and self-sacrifice are admirable. The agent-relative bias we've just considered can agree with that, but—if it gives Fred's own interest enough weight—it can't agree that Fred did the thing there was most reason for him to do. If it allocates enough strength to Fred's own interest, it will hold that there was in fact more reason, or at least as much reason, for him to take evasive action. This view can accept that he

---

[21] Here I assume that one should do what one has a moral obligation to do.

[22] This is in line with the indeterminacy view suggested by Phillips.

showed courage and self-sacrifice, but—inasmuch as he showed it in pursuit of what he took to be the thing there was most reason to do—it also has to hold that he acted from a mistake, whereas Fred might well have thought there was point to this courage and self-sacrifice *only* if this was *the* thing there was most reason to do. I find myself on the side of Fred. It seems to me that he was not mistaken in his motivating thought—that falling on the grenade was what there was most reason for him to do. Though he went beyond the call of duty he acted for the best, and he showed courage and self-sacrifice in doing so. No doubt I would have been among those taking evasive action; however, I don't claim either that that would have been the *best* thing for me to do or that it would have been the thing there was *most reason* for me to do.

4. *Practical reasons and their sources*

To move forward we need to consider the various sources from which reasons for acting derive. In particular, we need to consider the way in which reasons to feel give rise to reasons to act.

Consider again the case of gratitude. Out of sheer goodness of heart, someone does me an unrequested good turn. That fact certainly gives me reason to feel grateful. And because I have reason to feel grateful to him for his good turn, I have reason to express that gratitude, for example by thanking him or giving him a present or by returning the favour. Suppose on the other hand that he did me some undeserved harm. In that case I have good reason to feel resentful. And because I have reason to feel resentment I have reason to express that resentment, by recrimination, insistence on apology or even by seeking compensation.

These connections between reasons to feel and reasons to act are examples of what I have elsewhere called the 'Feeling/Disposition Principle': 'If there's reason to feel ϕ there's reason to do what feeling ϕ characteristically disposes one to do.'[23] And I think one can say that

---

[23] *Ethical Explorations*. By the characteristic disposition of a feeling I mean not just any action it causes but the action it functions to cause. For example, fear functions to cause flight, though it may cause one to be rooted to the spot.

the practical reasons generated by this principle do not stem from practical reason, at least when 'practical reason' is understood in a fairly common, narrow way: let us say, from 'pure practical reason'. It's not pure practical reason that tells me that if I have suffered a harm— even one that was unintended by the harmer—I have reason to demand an apology.[24] About this kind of normative knowledge rationalism is hardly plausible. What I need to understand, rather, is something about the hermeneutics of two emotions, resentment and regret. I need to understand that an undeserved harm can be an appropriate object of resentment on the part of the person harmed, and further, that when a person feels reasonable resentment towards me, then it is reasonable for me to feel sorry and to express that feeling by apologising to him and if necessary by reparation.

I could not know these vital normative truths (other than by testimony) if I did not myself have feelings of resentment and regret. That's what I mean when I say that these truths belong to the hermeneutics of these emotions. To know them I must know what resentment and regret are— know it, so to speak, from within. Pure practical reason can't tell me that, by definition, since by 'pure practical reason', or 'practical reason' used narrowly, we mean a faculty which enables us to recognise reasons irrespective of our capacity to feel emotions and thus to know what they are. This also means that the Feeling/Disposition Principle is not a principle of pure practical reason, since we know it by knowing its instances, and these are intelligible only to those capable of the relevant feeling.

But now consider the special case of desire. The desire for an object is a feeling whose characteristic disposition is: trying to get that object. So it falls under the Feeling/Disposition Principle in the following way:

(D) If there is reason for you to desire x then there is reason for you to obtain, achieve, bring about x.

In this principle the notion of what there is reason for you to desire is not to be understood instrumentally, that is, as what there is reason to

---

[24] This principle is only roughly stated. If you beat me in an important competition you may in one sense at least harm me but you don't have to apologise (though you might say that you're sorry that only one of us could win, and so on).

desire because it satisfies some more basic desire. Rather, the notion invokes a distinction between reasonable and unreasonable desires—in line with the distinction between reasonable and unreasonable gratitude, resentment, envy, admiration, annoyance and so forth. In all of these cases we can often judge that a particular feeling would in a particular situation have been reasonable or unreasonable—whether or not the person in question actually felt that way. For example, it would have been quite reasonable for you to feel resentment; there was good reason for you to feel it—whether or not you felt it. A desire can be reasonable or unreasonable in the same non-instrumental way. For example, there's good reason for you to want that particular cake on the tray—you particularly enjoy chocolate cakes and that's a good one.[25] And just as reasonable gratitude or resentment rationalise their characteristic disposition, so reasonable desire rationalises its characteristic disposition. Notice that (D) is only a conditional, not a biconditional. I am not saying that you've got reason to obtain, achieve, or bring about x *only* if you've got reason to desire x. There may well be things you have reason to do which you don't have any non-instrumental reason to desire to do, such as throwing yourself on the grenade—indeed there often are.

So desire falls under the Feeling/Disposition Principle. But I also said it was a special case. One way in which it's special, which is particularly relevant to the present discussion, is by dint of its special connection to the notion of a person's good. It can be argued that the notion of a person, N's, good is definable as that which there is reason for N to desire. If this definition is right, then (E) reduces to (D). Or rather it reduces to the following, strengthened, version of (D).

> (D′) If there is reason for N to desire x to a given degree then there is reason of proportionate degree for N to obtain, achieve, bring about x.

On this definition of a person's good the egoist's principle reduces to a special case of the Feeling/Disposition Principle. And that means that

---

[25] Your desire for that particular piece of cake need not be instrumental to a desire for—that is, it need not be a 'means to'—your own enjoyment, as has long been pointed out: for example by Bishop Butler, or J. S. Mill.

its source is not pure practical reason, but the hermeneutics of desire. Moreover, it can at least be argued that Sidgwick himself defined a person's good as what there is reason for that person to desire.[26] So Sidgwick too could accept the reduction of egoism to the Feeling/Disposition Principle.

But further, on this definition of a person's good we can also rewrite (I), the principle which stated that 'the fact that an action will promote to some degree the good of beings overall, taking the good of all beings into account by some impartial principle, gives anyone a reason of proportionate degree to do that action'. The good of a being, on this definition, is whatever it is that that being has reason to desire. So what (I) is saying is that if an action x, which is open to you, would promote to some degree something which some being N has reason to desire, then you have some reason to do x. How strong the reason is will depend on how strong N's reason to desire the thing is, and how much effect, positive or negative, doing x would have on what other beings have reason to desire—taking the strength of their reasons to desire into account and computing it all by some impartial distributive principle.

Can (I) be said to be a principle of pure practical reason? That depends on how strongly one takes the notion of pure practical reason. Perhaps a principle of pure practical reason should not refer to *any* notion of what there is reason to feel—including what there is reason to *desire*—at all. Kant might insist on that, since the Categorical Imperative, derived as he envisages from the very notion of a reason for acting, makes no reference to what there is reason to feel. Correspondingly, it makes no reference to the notion of a person's good, which, we have argued, is indeed to be understood in terms of a notion of evaluative, as against practical, reason—namely the notion of what there is reason for that person to desire.

But non-Kantians are likely to feel that this is so strict a notion of pure practical reason as to be empty. So I propose a less strict notion. A principle of pure practical reason can make reference to the notion of what there is reason for an individual to desire, and hence to the notion

---

[26] See *Methods*, Bk I, ch. IX, sect 3. But see Skorupski, *Ethical Explorations*, 120, n. 23, and Skorupski, 'Desire and Will in Sidgwick and Green', *Utilitas*, 12 (2000): 316–17.

of an individual's good, but not to any other notion of what there is reason to feel. That means that on our analysis both (E) and (I) can be principles of pure practical reason. But are they?

I have already argued that (E) can be seen instead as a case of the Feeling/Disposition Principle. But (I) is different. The significant point about it is that it introduces a requirement of impartiality: it is this that takes it out of the realm of evaluative reasons into the realm of pure practical reason. There is, (I) says, reason for anyone impartially to promote the good of everyone. Famously, according to Sidgwick, this can be seen to be true 'from the point of view of the Universe'—and he has been well mocked for saying so.[27] But he could in my view rightly have said that it is true from the standpoint of pure practical reason—from the standpoint that is, for example, required in one's capacity as a citizen, as against the standpoint of the concretely situated individual with this or that specific endowment of affective dispositions triggered appropriately to that situation.

5. *Warrant and defeasibility*

(I), then, is a principle of pure practical reason; (E) is not. Thus there is no dualism of pure practical reason in the way in which Sidgwick envisages. But both (I) and (E), according to what has been said so far, are 'self-evident'—in that each has its own underived a priori warrant. So what happens if they come into conflict? Do we add them up or does one trump the other?

Here I can only speak for myself, certainly not for Sidgwick. It seems to me that it is the impartial principle that is finally determinative of the strength of reasons. And when its determinations can be known, they are the last court of appeal. To go back to the case of the grenade. Fred certainly has reason to desire to save himself, and everyone else in the dug-out has reason to desire to save themselves too. So

---

[27] See Bernard Williams, 'The point of view of the universe: Sidgwick and the ambitions of ethics', in his *Making Sense of Humanity* (Cambridge: Cambridge University Press, 1995): 153–71.

by (D'), that is (E), each can rightly conclude that he has reason to save himself. Is this reason, the reason from (E), somehow added to the reason from (I), so that each of the soldiers has most reason to fall to the ground, or even most reason to run away? I have already suggested that it isn't. Fred might think as follows:

> We all of us have a fundamental reason to pursue our own good, and what's more it often isn't clear what action would best promote the good of all. But here it's clear. And when it's clear what best promotes the good of all then that *is* what one has most reason to do—though not necessarily the morally obligatory thing to do.

If that's what Fred thinks, then he seems to me to think truly.

(I) is not just immediately warranted—it's indefeasible. The same, I suggest, cannot be said of (E). Suppose circumstances make it reasonable for me to feel gratitude to someone and to thank them, or to feel resentment and demand an apology. However, suppose it's also clear in the circumstances that the general good will be served if I don't thank or demand an apology. Then it's plausible to hold that the reason to thank or to demand apology is overruled (though the reason to *feel* grateful or resentful is not). These reasons for action, then, are defeated by (I). Suppose on the other hand that, in the circumstances, it's not the *general* good but *my own* interest that is best served if I don't thank or demand an apology. Then it's not clear that the reason to thank or demand an apology is overruled. Here two instances of the Feeling/Disposition Principle clash. I may feel, at least to some point, that there's more reason to show gratitude than to pursue my own best interest. Or I may feel that honour requires an apology even though I see that self-interest is somewhat better served by silently accepting the insult. And I may be right. Such reasons, then, are not automatically defeated by (E).

Finally we must bring back into the picture the concepts of moral obligation and blame. It would be wrong for the soldiers to run away from the dug-out when the grenade is thrown in, but it is not wrong for them to take evading action by falling to the floor. So Fred goes beyond the call of duty in falling on the grenade. If this is what we think, then we think that any soldier who runs away is blameworthy, but that a soldier who falls to the floor is not. Obviously Fred is not blameworthy either, so the moral obligation is disjunctive: either fall to the floor or fall on the grenade. The supererogatory element in Fred's act is that he chooses the second disjunct.

Moral wrongness, as thus illustrated, turns on blameworthiness—on what there is reason to blame. The core of blame is a certain complex of feeling—let us just call it 'the blame-feeling'. If resentment's characteristic disposition is recrimination and a call for reparation, the blame-feeling's characteristic disposition is the act of blame and the call for punishment or repentance. Just like all other feelings, the blame-feeling has its reasons which do not come from pure practical reason. But can we say that there is no connection at all between pure practical reason and the reasonableness of the blame-feeling? Compare the case of annoyance. Whether it's reasonable to be annoyed by something—a recalcitrant nail, scratching on a blackboard—is not a matter of pure practical reason at all (though of course whether it's reasonable, taking everything into account, to *act* on that annoyance may be, as we have noted). Can we say the same about the blame-feeling?

To answer this question we would have to take up some other issues in the hermeneutics of the blame-feeling. In particular we would have to ask whether it can ever be the case that a person has most reason to do something that's morally wrong. If the answer to this is, as I think it is, no, that must mean that questions about moral wrongness and questions about what impartiality requires can't be as divorced as questions about what is annoying and questions about what impartiality requires are. For, on that view, if (I) entails that some action is the one the agent has most reason to do, it will also entail that it can't be morally wrong for the agent to do it, and so entail that the agent can't be *blameworthy* in doing it. An action done because the agent reasonably thinks it is required by (I) can't be morally wrong, though such an action can certainly be 'prudentially wrong'. Hence it can't be reasonable to feel the blame-feeling towards such an action, and so considerations of pure practical reason can enter into the reasonableness of the blame-feeling. None the less it remains true that our ordinary moral intuitions are 'immediate' intuitions about blameworthiness. They are not *derived* from (I), though they are *corrigible* by (I).

6. *Conclusion*

To sum up, contrary to Sidgwick, there is no dualism of pure practical reason. Pure practical reason simply says that the good of any being is agent-neutrally good. On the other hand, if what we're talking about is not just pure practical reason but practical reasons in general, that is reasons for action, then there are many, and not just two. Under the Feeling/Disposition Principle an irreducible variety of reasonable feelings gives rise to an irreducible variety of underived reasons to act. Egoism has no special authority to overrule any of these practical reasons; properly understood it is simply a special case of them. On the other hand, both morality and the impartial principle have that authority; they can overrule reasons that come from the Feeling/Disposition Principle. And the impartial principle has a further authority over judgements about what there is reason to blame, which I have only alluded to briefly. What I have suggested in this case is that our judgements of blameworthiness do not *derive* from impartial reason, but that they stand open to correction by impartial reason, in a way that judgements about what is annoying, admirable, desirable for oneself and so on do not.

So Sidgwick was right to connect common-sense morality with the impartial principle; it's also understandable that he should be cagy about how it derives from that principle. However, it would be wrong to characterise this connection by saying that ordinary moral intuition cannot constitute *knowledge* until its content is derived from the impartial principle. Ordinary moral intuition can deliver immediately warranted judgements. Such moral judgements are, as a matter of general epistemological principle, defeasible, as indeed ordinary perceptual judgements are. But unless the truth of fallibilism about a domain is inconsistent with our having knowledge in that domain, there is no reason to deny that ordinary moral intuition can also deliver knowledge.

Sidgwick on Practical Reason[1]

ONORA O'NEILL

1. *How many methods?*

IN *THE METHODS OF ETHICS* Henry Sidgwick distinguishes *three* methods of ethics but (he claims) only *two* conceptions of practical reason. This may seem surprising. What is the difference between methods of ethics and procedures of practical reason supposed to be? Isn't the proper method for ethics the use of practical reason? John Skorupski addresses these issues with several interesting claims, and concludes that there is no dualism of practical reason: if practical reason is construed broadly there is pluralism; if construed narrowly there is a single principle.

As a preliminary to this argument Skorupski comments on Sidgwick's views of intuitionism. Sidgwick denies that intuitions provide practical reasons not because he thinks they must be common-sense judgements. On the contrary, he sees that the intuitions that would be most impor- tant for ethics would be not merely *underived* (which judgements of common sense are) but also immediate, clear, precise, even a priori and above all self-evident (which common-sense judgements are not) (7, 32). Skorupski suggests that Sidgwick thought that there is no principle of practical reason corresponding to intuitionism because there are no intuitions of this more fundamental sort. Seemingly this should resolve the problem of Sidgwick holding that there are three methods

---

[1] All notes are given parenthetically, with edition and page number, and are to Henry Sidgwick, *The Methods of Ethics* (Indianapolis, Indiana: Hackett, 1981). This edition, which contains a foreword by John Rawls, is a facsimile of the 1907 seventh edition, which contains the prefaces of all editions of the text.

Proceedings of the British Academy, **109**, 83–89. © The British Academy 2001.

of ethics but only two principles of practical reason. But the discrep-
ancy between *three* methods and *two* principles of practical reason may
arise because the intuitionist does not derive moral claims from anything else, so gets by without needing any principle of practical reason.
This thought seems plausible because practical reason, whatever else it
may be used for, supports derivations. It would be redundant if ethics
could draw on underived intuitive claims, whatever their source.
Intuitions may (if they exist) provide a method of ethics, but they do not
do so by providing a form of practical reasoning.

However, this neat resolution does not fit with much else in
Sidgwick's text. For it seems that the difference between the egoist and
the impartialist (the utilitarian) also may not be a difference about
practical reason. Egoist and impartialist alike can, it seems, accept a
principle of practical reason, namely the principle that 'whatever is
right for me is right for all persons in all circumstances' (7, xvii). As
Skorupski points out, this suggests that there is just one method of
practical reason, shared by egoist and impartialist alike, so yielding
three methods of ethics (intuitionism, egoism and or impartialism
(utilitarianism)), but *one* principle of practical reason.

Yet unless egoism and impartialism are given very weak interpre-
tations, they conflict, and if they agree about practical reason, that
conflict will not be susceptible of rational resolution. Egoists and
impartialists will find themselves uncongenial passengers on the same
boat: neither will be able to persuade the other on disputed points. The
antinomy (Kant) or dualism (Hegel) of duty and self-interest, of virtue
and happiness, of morality and nature is not dispelled by practical
reason.

What differentiates the egoist and the impartialist is then not their
view of the principle 'whatever is right for me is right for all persons in
all circumstances', which Sidgwick calls 'the Kantian maxim' and
thinks 'fundamental, certainly true and not without practical importance' (7, xix). It is their view of the good. As I read Sidgwick, he does
not use the Kantian phrases 'practical reason' and 'pure practical
reason' to refer to the various claims about the good which distinguish
different methods of ethics, but to a common core that all methods of
ethics apart from intuitionism deploy. That is why he concludes that

'the Kantian maxim' cannot determine which method of ethics we have reason to adopt, and (reluctantly) that utilitarianism too must have its basis in intuition. In the Preface to the sixth edition of *The Methods of Ethics* he confesses: 'I was then a Utilitarian again, but on an Intuitional basis' (7, xxi–xxii). For Sidgwick, practical reason guides the process by which those who are committed to one or another view of the good reach claims about obligation and duty. It cannot supply reasons for adopting any specific account of the good, and so is not or at least is only part of a method of ethics. If Sidgwick's account of practical reason cannot tell us which conception of the good to adopt, what does it provide?

2. *Practical reason in* The Methods of Ethics

It is by no means easy to be sure in the complex argument of *The Methods of Ethics* how much Sidgwick offers by way of an account of practical reason. Perhaps the easiest point to be sure about is his view of the *function* of practical reason. He holds that a method of ethics is 'any rational procedure by which we determine what individual human beings ought to do' (7, 1). Ethics is essentially practical: 'an attempt to ascertain the general laws or uniformities by which the varieties of human conduct ... may be *explained* is essentially different from an attempt to determine which among these varieties of conduct is *right*' (7, 2; cf. 7, 5; 7, 15). Practical reason is reasoning deployed *assuming some method of ethics* (an account of the good) to identify the right, and 'wrong conduct is essentially irrational' (7,23; cf. 7,35). (There is in my view some tension between this central aim and the comparativist ambitions which guide the composition of *The Methods of Ethics*.)

Ethics 'as the study of what is right or what ought to be' (7, 4) will differ depending on which view is taken—'ends accepted as ultimate or paramount', or whether it is independent of such ends. It is the diversity of possible ends 'accepted as ultimate' which explains how there can be a plurality of methods of ethics: 'to every difference in the end adopted at least some difference in method will generally correspond'

(7, 8). In short, on Sidgwick's account, methods of ethics, although not differentiated by the conception of practical reason they deploy, are distinguished but by the end(s), which they view as ultimate and paramount (7, 8). We may view either happiness or excellence (perfection) as the ultimate end, and if we think happiness is paramount we may then differ over whether universal or individual happiness should be preferred. In principle Sidgwick thinks that there might be a lot of methods of ethics (but not, contra Skorupski, lots of principles of practical reason). In practice he doubts whether there are serious contenders other than intuitionistic perfectionism, egoism, and impartialism (utilitarianism).

Despite these basically teleological views, Sidgwick argues in *The Methods of Ethics* (7, ch. III) that *right* is the fundamental ethical category. He writes that 'the fundamental notion represented by the word "ought" or "right" ... [is] essentially different from all notions representing physical or psychical experience' (7, 25) (so rejecting naturalism and psychologism); that it is not generally to be identified with the idea of fitness for purpose (7, 26) (some acts are unconditionally right); that it is not to be identified with and does not express feelings of approbation (7, 27–8). He argues explicitly of '"ought", "right" and other terms expressing the same fundamental notion' that 'the notion which these terms have in common is too elementary to admit of a formal definition'. He even uses the Kantian vocabulary and makes claims about *unconditional* or *categorical imperatives* (7, 35). However, Sidgwick's use of this vocabulary is remote from Kant's thought: in speaking of certain obligations as categorical he means only that they do not depend on the existence of any non-rational desires; such obligations may yet depend on an account of the good. The Kantian vocabulary of reason is put to use in the framework of a teleological ethics.

This fact makes it puzzling that Sidgwick so often writes as if he accepted Kant's conception of practical reason. I think the reason he does this is that what he terms 'the Kantian maxim' is a startlingly weak reading of Kant's principal conception of practical reason, with wide applicability but slender implications. When Sidgwick renders Kant's principle of practical reason merely as 'That whatever is right for me must be right for all persons in similar circumstances' (7, xix; see also

379–80), he notes (quite correctly) that this principle fails to decide matters as between self-interest and duty, between egoists and universalists. He does not ask whether this is an adequate or complete account of practical reason.

What Sidgwick terms 'the Kantian maxim' is in fact no more than a principle of universal generalisation applied within ethics; it is not Kant's universalisability test. No mention here of the requirement on agents to test whether they can will principles as a universal law; no mention of the double modal structure of Kantian universalisability which *requires* that agents act only on principles which they *can* will for all. No wonder Sidgwick concluded that the Kantian principle as he understood it was too weak 'for the construction of a system of duties' (7, xix), and that it offered no reason for preferring universalism to egoism, or (more broadly) duty to happiness. Equally he realised that the missing connections would not be established by the second conception of practical reason which he accepted, for this principle is simply Kant's principle of the hypothetical imperative—a version of the principle of instrumental reasoning (7, 37), which supports claims about what ought to be done that are 'implicitly relative to an *optional* end' (7, 7).

As Sidgwick relates his difficulties in the short essay in intellectual autobiography that is included within the Preface to the sixth edition of *The Methods of Ethics*, his growing realisation of the insufficiency of practical reason led him to 'reconsider his relation to Intuitional Ethics' (7, xxi). The reconsideration led in two directions. On the one hand it revealed that even egoism requires a basis in intuition: for why should the egoist pursue self-interest at the expense of immediate inclination? Rational egoism itself had its foundation in an intuited 'Axiom of Prudence ... a self-evident principle implied in rational egoism' (386). Axioms, of course, lack derivation.

His reflections also led him to the conviction that utilitarians too could not prove their basic principle and would have to invoke an intuited, self-evident 'Axiom of Benevolence'. Utilitarianism too relies on an intuited, underived 'axiom': 'That a rational agent is bound to aim at Universal Happiness' (7, xxi). Sidgwick found himself led back to a utilitarian substantive ethics not because he showed how practical reason could demonstrate the principle of utility, but because 'I am finally led to the conclusion ... that the Intuitional method rigorously applied yields as its final result the doctrine of ... Utilitarianism' (7, 407), a doctrine within which his two principles of practical reason can be applied. He had found himself unable to reach any resolution of the conflicts between egoism and impartialism, let alone of the more fundamental differences between interest and duty, nature and morality.

So what is the tally? Sidgwick can, I think, indeed allow for three and perhaps for many more methods of ethics, but what differentiates these methods is not the view that they take of practical reason, but the underlying intuitions about ultimate ends on which they build. He allows for two conceptions of practical reason, and assumes (in my view wrongly) that these correspond to Kant's categorical and hypothetical imperatives. His minimal formulation of a principle of practical reason, which he thinks corresponds to the categorical imperative, ensures that his account of practical reason *taken by itself* underdetermines not only ethical judgement, but also the methods and principles of ethics. These principles can be derived only by invoking methods whose epistemological footing lies in intuitions about the good.

The lingering sadness of so many passages in *The Methods of Ethics* reflects Sidgwick's dispassionate and stoical refusal to assert claims that cannot be supported by reasons and his view that practical reason supplies no more than universal generalisation and instrumental rationality. Although his discussion of practical reason is often conducted in Kant's terminology, it is profoundly unlike Kant's. Perhaps he thought that Kant's vindication of reason was too bound up with a theism for which he could find no adequate proof. Ironically the direction of Kant's argument is in fact the converse: from a view about practical reason to a conception of reasoned hope that can (but perhaps need not) be given a theistic reading. Kant's vindication of reason, by contrast, explicitly repudiates theistic assumptions. If it had presupposed theism, his discussions of reasoned hope, and of religion 'within the limits of mere reason', would presumably have been redundant.

In seeing practical reason as universal generalisation, a principle that is as useful to the egoist as to the impartialist, Sidgwick adopts a starkly individualistic view of reason. Like cases are to be treated alike, but nothing is said about a plurality of agents. A solitary individual seeking to impose reason on action can be guided by this principle (of course, the guidance will be weak). Kant's explicit view that practical reason asks what principles can or cannot be *willed* or *adopted* by *all agents* is missing. There is no consideration of universalisability, of the implications of the fact that reasons (whatever else they may be) must be followable by those to whom they are addressed. Of course, Kant's account of practical reason may be a failure. Its vindication may be problematic, and its power of resolution inadequate. But this is not shown by pointing out the slender implications of Sidgwick's weak reading of what he calls 'the Kantian maxim'.

SECTION III

The Sanctions of Utilitarianism[1]

ROSS HARRISON

LET ME START WITH A QUOTATION. See if you can place this. 'The question is often asked, and properly so, in regard to any supposed moral standard—What is its sanction? what are the motives to obey it? or more specifically, what is the source of its obligation? whence does it derive its binding force?' Now, given the context of this collection, if you didn't recognise the quotation, you might naturally have supposed that it was Sidgwick speaking. If so, you would have been wrong. It is in fact the first words of Chapter 3 of J. S. Mill's work, *Utilitarianism*, and the title of that chapter is 'On the ultimate sanction of the principle of utility'. So this is where Mill is concerned with what he calls the sanctions of utilitarianism; that is, with the topic of this paper. Now that you have located (or been confirmed in your knowledge) that it was Mill, you may well be thinking that, of course, it could not possibly have been Sidgwick. For Sidgwick was an internalist about moral motivation; that is, once we have identified the right thing to do, there need be no further question about how we are motivated to do it. As Sidgwick puts it in the 'Ethical Judgments' chapter of *The Methods of Ethics*, 'when I speak of the cognition or judgment that "X ought to be done" ... as a dictate or precept of reason ... I imply that in rational beings as such this cognition gives a motive or impulse to action' (VII, 34). So it would seem that Sidgwick could not have a problem about

---

[1] References to Sidgwick's *Methods of Ethics* give the number of the edition referred to in roman capital letters followed by the page number in that edition.

Proceedings of the British Academy, **109**, 93–116. © The British Academy 2001.

moral motive, and hence would not have worried about the sanctions of morality, or utilitarianism. Unlike Mill, it would seem that he could never have written a chapter about it.

This, however, would be too hasty. For the last chapter of the first edition of Sidgwick's *The Methods of Ethics* is entitled 'The sanctions of utilitarianism'; and it is from the title of Sidgwick's famous last chapter that I have lifted the title of this paper. Therefore Sidgwick as well as Mill discusses the sanctions of utilitarianism, and I want to examine this discussion both to investigate Sidgwick's relations to his utilitarian predecessors and also because it may cast light from an unusual direction on the famous end of the first edition of *The Methods of Ethics*. This is where Sidgwick gets caught in the dualism of practical reason and hence finds his whole work a self-confessed failure. If this dualism cannot be solved, then, as he puts it here, 'the Cosmos of Duty is thus really reduced to a Chaos: and the prolonged effort of the human intellect to frame a perfect ideal of rational conduct is seen to have been fore-doomed to inevitable failure' (I, 473).

Three years later, in his second edition, Sidgwick changed the chapter, dropping the title, the beginning, and the end. However, let us continue for the moment to look at it in its first-edition form, where it is a chapter which starts with the title 'The sanctions of utilitarianism' and ends with the word 'failure'. Sidgwick is, typically, more hesitant than Mill. Mill starts his chapter, as we saw, by saying that the question about sanctions is a proper question. Sidgwick starts his chapter by saying that 'We have now, perhaps, obtained a sufficiently clear outline of the manner in which a consistent Utilitarian will behave. But many persons will still feel that, after all, it has not really been shown why a man should be a consistent Utilitarian.' He then remarks that in an earlier chapter

> we seem to have proved ... that it is reasonable to take the Greatest Happiness of the Greatest Number as the ultimate end of action. But in order that this proof may have any practical effect, a man must have a certain impulse to do what is reasonable as such: and many persons will say—and probably with truth—that if such a wish exists in them at all it is feeble in comparison with other impulses: and that they require some much stronger inducement to do what is right than this highly abstract and refined desire.

That he has proved the truth of utilitarianism might well seem to be a sufficient answer to the question of why people should be utilitarians. Nevertheless Sidgwick gets involved with 'inducements', that is, with sanctions. Reasons have to be effective. Yet his interpolated 'and probably with truth' lacks the strength of Mill's brisk 'and properly so'. It remains somewhat open how seriously Sidgwick himself is involved with the problem of sanctions (as opposed to something which 'many persons will say').

Sanctions are referred to in fact much earlier in Sidgwick's great work, and also in all of its editions. If we go back to Chapter 5 of Book 2, we find a chapter which is called, in all editions, 'Happiness and duty'. Here Sidgwick talks about sanctions and in doing so he refers in all editions to Bentham. In the last editions he says, 'here it will be convenient to adopt with some modification the terminology of Bentham; and to regard the pleasures consequent on the conformity to moral rules, and the pains consequent on their violation, as the "sanctions" of these rules' (VII, 164). On terminology Sidgwick is correct. The language of 'sanctions' is pure Bentham. Chapter III of Bentham's major work, his *Introduction to the Principles of Morals and Legislation*, which is the first chapter after his statement and defence of the principle of utility, is entitled 'Of the four sanctions or sources of pain and pleasure'. So now we have another sanctions chapter; that is, all three members of the Holy Trinity of English Utilitarianism, Bentham, Mill, and Sidgwick, wrote a chapter on its sanctions. The four sanctions Bentham lists here are here called the 'physical'; the 'political'; the 'moral or popular'; and the 'religious' sanctions. Later, for example in his map of all possible motives called *The Springs of Action Tables*, Bentham added a fifth sanction, the sympathetic sanction. But the strongest and most important sanctions are the four he cites in the *Introduction* and throughout his life. In each case the name indicates the source of the motivating pleasure and pain. The physical sanction is the pure physical consequences of an action, so that my anticipation of a hangover may be a sanction or motive controlling the amount I drink. 'Political' for Bentham means a legal sanction, that is penalties artificially attached by law to kinds of action hence forming additional motives for people not to do them. So, to stay with drunkenness, there might be laws against drunkenness threatening fines or imprisonment for being drunk, and hence giving a motive for not drinking. By 'moral or popular' Bentham means public opinion, that is the inconveniences into which I would run by doing those things which are publicly disapproved, such as being drunk in the street. Bentham calls this the 'moral' sanction, but, as Mill later sniffily commented on and criticised (in his 'Bentham' essay), Bentham does not take morality itself to provide a sanction. The incentives are not, that is, taken to come from one's own moral sense but, rather, from other people's. Lastly Bentham has the 'religious' sanction, which is the penalties annexed to actions by the divine law-giver, so if God were to tell me, for example, that drunkenness leads to hell-fire, this would be an additional sanction against drinking too much; it would, that is, give me another reason for not getting drunk.

This is Bentham, whom as we have seen is woven into Sidgwick's text. Bentham particularly appears in the first (as I say, in the *Introduction*), more historically oriented, edition and here Bentham is much admired. When, for example, Sidgwick dismisses Bentham's posthumous *Deontology* as really being a work of Bentham's own pen, he does so because he finds in it things which, as he puts it, are 'impossible to attribute to so exact and coherent a thinker as Bentham' (II, 68). So Bentham is taken to be exact and coherent. Sidgwick is also exact, even if, attempting a wider range, he is not quite so coherent. He is particularly exact, I think, in the much longer passage which in the earlier editions stands in the place of the short summary about Bentham and sanctions which I quoted. Here Sidgwick says,

> It has been already observed, that while stating General Happiness as the right and proper end of conduct, Bentham still regarded it as natural and normal for each agent to aim at his own individual happiness. He therefore considered human pleasure (and pain as its negative quantity) from two quite distinct points of view: first as constituting the end and standard of right conduct, and so determining the rules which Bentham and other rational philanthropists would desire to be generally obeyed in any community: and secondly as constituting the motives (whether pleasures or pains) by which each member of the community is or may be induced to conform to these rules. (I, 148)

Then he starts to classify what he calls 'these Motives or Sanctions' in a way which is also common to the later editions.

I think that this is exactly right as a description of Bentham. The fact that, as Sidgwick elsewhere puts it, 'there is ... in Bentham's mind no confusion and no logical connexion between his psychological generalization and his ethical assumption' is both crucial and also frequently overlooked. We can see the distinction at the start of Bentham's 'Sanctions' chapter where Bentham says 'Having taken a general view of these two grand objects (viz. pleasure, and what comes to the same thing, immunity from pain) in the character of *final* causes; it will be necessary to take a view of pleasure and pain itself, in the character of *efficient* causes, or means' (III, 1). In other words, after showing what ought to be done in his chapters on utility (the final causes) Bentham now turns in his 'Sanctions' chapter to how it may be done. As well as ends, there are means; as well as what Sidgwick called in that long quoted passage the 'end and standard of right conduct' there is what Sidgwick called there the 'motives ... by which each member of the community is or may be induced to conform to these rules'.

Indeed, Bentham's whole project only makes sense if such a fundamental distinction between psychology and ethics is made. For Bentham's project is precisely to take people as they actually are and then to see what system of government and legislation is required to make them do what they ought to do. The idea is, as Bentham puts it, to 'promote the happiness of the society, by punishing and rewarding' (*Introduction*, VII, 1). That is, the correct evaluative end, which is the happiness of society, is to be provided by appealing to people's self-interested motives, using threats of pain or hopes of pleasure, that is, using punishment and reward. The legislator therefore needs to know both the value theory and also the psychological reality of people in order to know which sanctions should be applied to which people to get them to do which things. General happiness comes from people not stealing, so punishments are fixed for theft, forming a sanction against bad behaviour. The same applies in Bentham to the proper structure of organisations and, indeed, the construction of government itself. Bentham's panopticon prison, to take a famous example, is precisely meant to be a physical or spatial solution to the question of how the self-interested prisoners are to be motivated to do what they ought; but the same applies to the problem of who guards its guards, the principles of management by which its self-interested governor is to be motivated to run the prison properly.

What we get in Bentham, then, is a political solution to a moral problem. Theft is bad; people do not do as they ought. The solution is to have law and government, which by imposition of the so-called 'political' sanction makes it in people's interests not to steal. Other sanctions are involved, for as Bentham says, the political sanction involves the physical; the physical walls of the prison are part of the deterrent for bad behaviour. Also, as Bentham says in his 'Sanctions' chapter, the legislator overlooks the religious and social sanction at his peril. And as well as what Bentham calls direct legislation, there is what he calls indirect legislation, that is, the other ways than punishment by which a legislator can influence or educate people. However, the whole work is written from the perspective of the legislator.

It is therefore a political solution to a moral problem. It is what a legislator does; or, more accurately, what a good legislator should do. However, the present question, or the question of Mill's and Sidgwick's 'Sanctions' chapters, is whether the same can be done for morality; done for morality, that is, without using legislation. Where the texts of the early and late editions join, Sidgwick next says that the 'sanctions we may classify as External and Internal'. External is like Bentham; and Sidgwick here identifies what he calls 'Legal Sanctions' and also 'Social Sanctions'. (So Sidgwick's 'legal' corresponds to Bentham's 'legal or political', and Sidgwick's 'social' corresponds to Bentham's 'popular or moral'.) However, when Sidgwick mentions 'internal' sanctions, he becomes more like Mill than Bentham. In Mill's 'Sanctions' chapter, with which I started, he also says that 'sanctions are either external or internal' and indeed he spends much more time on the internal sanctions than the external, that is on how I feel when I do wrong and so on. Now this might be thought to be the clue we need as to how we can find sanctions for morality. As well as the pains of the externally imposed law we have the pains of the inner conscience. Sidgwick, for example, notes here that 'The internal sanctions of duty … will lie in the pleasurable emotion attending virtuous action, or in the absence of remorse' (VII, 164). This might seem like the clue. But in fact internal sanctions do not make the problem different in any fundamental way. Bentham may have been criticised by Mill for leaving them out, but as long as the pains of conscience are taken as merely unpleasant feelings, like having a bad stomach ache, they operate in the same way as the externals: the anticipated hangover may stop me drinking; the anticipated misery of remorse may stop me breaking my promise.

Another way of putting the point is to say that there is in Bentham no problem about moral agency. All agency for him is purely self-interested and so the solution to the problem of morality is purely political. Once the political is taken away, it is not clear what a purely moral problem and solution would be. We would just have people acting, and by luck or divine intervention happening or otherwise unintentionally to hit the right target. However, at least unless we are God, there is nothing that can be done about it. And even if we are God (or introduce God), we have another politician, a divine legislator, who, by keeping the home fires of hell burning bright, manages to get people to do the right thing.

At first sight, therefore, there could not be for Bentham a purely moral analogue to the problems to be solved by legislation. Legislation is an art, a form of cooking in which the right cake is to be made with these ingredients. But, take away the political machinery and there seems nothing left to do; no comparable purely moral task. However, even on Bentham's own account, this cannot be quite right. As well as what the cooks cook, there is the question why they cook what they do. In other words we have the question of the legislators' own motives for action. Why are they attempting to achieve the greatest happiness of the greatest number; and if they are, are they not being moral in a way that the psychology cannot explain? The account is of what a legislator should do, and this does not make sense unless there is scope for the legislator to make morally motivated choices. There is also the problem of Bentham's own position, that is of the philanthropic adviser to the legislator who explains how the legislator should act to get general happiness. Bentham himself seems to be acting in a morally motivated manner, for, as Mill pointed out in his 'Bentham' essay, Bentham was himself very unlike the self-interested operators whom he took as the typical or universal specimens of human activity.

There do therefore seem to be exceptions to Bentham's psychological claim that people are animals which act in a universally self-interested manner. Bentham in fact sometimes allows this. And Sidgwick in the long comment which I quoted says merely that Bentham regarded it as 'natural and normal' for each agent to aim at their own happiness. However, Bentham did usually claim it as a universal truth (and is quoted by Sidgwick elsewhere as doing so). And when Sidgwick produced the second edition of *The Methods of Ethics*, he left the long passage I quoted alone except that for 'natural and normal' he substituted 'every human agent actually does aim at his own individual happiness' (II, 148). However, either way, it does not spoil Bentham's legislative project, his cook's task, because for this, knowledge of general rather than of universal behaviour is sufficient. As long as you know that in general people do not want to go to prison, you can institute this as a sanction to deter theft and its efficacy won't be much undermined by occasional monkish characters who find prison an answer to their spiritual needs.

Bentham still has to give some explanation of why he himself (apparently altruistically) advises legislators and also why any legislator (apparently altruistically) should listen to the advice. As for himself, his explanation is that he just happens to be one of those people who are not motivated in a narrowly self-interested sense; or (the trivial form of this) who get their happiness from doing good to others. As for the legislator he is attempting to advise, presumably the strategy is just to wait for one which happens, by the same exceptional chance, to look benevolent. Then when you get her, a Catherine the Great of Russia perhaps, you head for Russia and start writing advice.

This may not be inconsistent. However, it is very risky. Benevolent dictators are still dictators, and if they institute the perfect system of law on Monday they may still hang you without trial on Friday. So a better answer is the one which Bentham came up with later in his life. This is to have a political system which will automatically, in its normal process of running, produce the good. The system is democracy. Here, again, we put together the separate psychological and ethical principles to achieve the result. The ethical principles state that the consequence which ought to emerge is the greatest happiness of the greatest number. The psychological principles state that people in fact aim at their own happiness. Therefore the greatest number will in fact aim at the happiness of the greatest number. Therefore putting the greatest number in charge (as happens in majoritarian democracy) means that people following their normal psychological courses will happen to come up with the goods. The moral problem of getting the right thing done is again solved politically; the political system ensures success.

We have now got rid of the legislator who has to be heroically moral, or otherwise has uncertain motivations. Merely moral motivation is no longer required. Instead the sanctions are provided by a machine which runs by itself, just as Bentham's panopticon prison is designed as a machine to run by itself, a machine to produce moral good without moral motivation. Normal psychological sanctions are sufficient and the job is all done by possible pains. This is again a political solution. However, it now seems that we could describe something similar for morality without involving the political. For when we have a machine that runs by itself we no longer have the cooks. The Benthamite philosopher is no longer an adviser on how to bake cakes but merely a commentator on the fact that the machine in its normal workings seems to be producing the good.

However, if mere commentary is all that is possible, then it would seem that exactly the same could be done for morals independently of politics. It could be pointed out in a precisely analogous way that the workings of the normal human psychology happen by and large to produce the right moral consequences. This could be taken to have divine backing, as with the theological utilitarians from Cumberland to Paley. The benevolent God is taken to have so fixed our psychology that (by and large) acting on our normal impulses means that we end up with the greatest good. This can also be given an invisible-handed economic spin whereby God (no doubt with time off after fixing physics) benevolently fixed the truth of general equilibrium theory so that satisfying our individual desires is again all for the best. However, even with the ruthlessly secular utilitarians such as Mill (and Spencer or Leslie

Stephen) the long-run experience of evolving humanity has given us a useful nature, so that by following our natural desires we are happening also to be producing general good. So we reach again Mill's 'Sanctions' chapter. But so also, it would seem, we may reach Sidgwick's 'Sanctions' chapter. We may, that is, now have this chapter in precisely the way it is, starting with sanctions and ending with the dualism of practical reason.

For the question now is whether people acting self-interestedly nevertheless happen to produce the right moral consequences. And, as long as there is a large overlap between what you will arrive at if you act self-interestedly and what you will arrive at if you act benevolently, then there are indeed sanctions to be moral. And such an overlap is precisely something that Sidgwick argues for in this chapter. Even if people are normally or universally the self-interested machines portrayed by Bentham, nevertheless they will still do those things which as a consequence produce the right results. They will, that is, produce the same things as they would have produced if they had instead been acting on benevolent, universal, reasons. It is exactly the same as the democratic story: morality is the unintended consequence of the normal self-interested working of the machine. Of course it is not automatic or guaranteed. Occasionally there will be divergence. But on the whole the machine works. The cakes are made but nobody intends to cook.

Alternatively, we might be less sanguine about there being a large overlap between what naturally arises from self-interested motivation and what would arise from universal benevolence. However, it would seem that we could still put the point as follows. Either self-interested and benevolent reasons agree in their practical effects or they do not. If they agree, then we have self-interested reasons to be moral, hence solving the sanctions of utilitarianism problem, and hence also show-ing that the supposed problem of dualism of reason is merely apparent. Alternatively, they do not agree. Then we are into problems on both counts. Sanctions cannot now be reliably presented for being utilitarian and we are also into deep difficulties over the dualism. Sidgwick points out in the course of the chapter that although there is normal coinci-dence, there is both possible and actual divergence. For him, doing the right thing may not be in our interest or make us happy, whereas, as he puts it in a footnote, 'some few thoroughly selfish persons appear at least to be happier than most of the unselfish' (1, 464n). So morality may well not be good for you. The course is set for the final failure whereby the cosmos of duty cracks apart into chaos; but this failure will also be a failure for the topic with which the chapter starts, that is with finding the sanctions of utilitarianism.

All this would seem to support Sidgwick's apparent strategy of writing a chapter about sanctions and ending up discussing the dualism of the practical reason. However, it is not in fact this simple; and it is not simple for reasons which Sidgwick himself brought out in his discussion of what he calls psychological hedonism, that is, the psychology of both Bentham and Mill. For Sidgwick there are two things wrong with Mill's famous proof of utilitarianism: the premiss and the inference. The premiss is that happiness is the only thing aimed at as an ultimate end; the inference is that therefore this is the right and proper end of conduct, the thing at which we ought to be aiming. The criticism of the inference, of the move from *is* to *ought*, is a criticism of a mistake which Sidgwick thinks Mill made but which, as we have seen, he thinks that Bentham never made, holding as Bentham does the descriptive psychology quite distinct from the evaluative ethics. However, both Bentham and Mill share what I have called the premiss of Mill's argument, and this also Sidgwick criticises. Sidgwick points out that people do not only aim at their own pleasure. People may, for example, be concerned with things which happen after their death, when they are no longer around to experience anything or have any pleasure. More generally, Sidgwick shows that desire is not necessarily a desire for pleasure. My hunger makes me desire food, but this desire is not a desire for the pleasure which the food may give. Indeed, in what Sidgwick calls the paradox of hedonism, it may be that the best way to get pleasure is not explicitly to pursue it. What all this means is that the things which Bentham holds together come apart: that is, desire, motivation, anticipation of pleasure, sanctions.

The title of Bentham's 'Sanctions' chapter was the 'sanctions or sources of pain and pleasure'. We have just seen that sanctions, that is Bentham's pleasure and pain, are not the only motives to action. But even

if they were, or when they are, how on the Benthamite account are they
meant to work? That is, how is the pain supposed to connect with the
action? A present pain may explain present action; but most of the action
supposedly explained by sanctions is explained by possible future pains,
such as threats of punishment. Here it is not the fact of the future pain
that is meant to explain motivation and action but, rather, my anticipation of it. Unknown pains will not motivate, yet I can be motivated by
false expectations. Hence it is not the pleasures and pains in themselves
that do the work but how they seem to me. But these may diverge; I can
make mistakes. One example of this, which Bentham notices, but which
is particularly important for Sidgwick, is in my estimation of the value
of future pains. Our psychological practice is to discount them, so that
the further off they are in the future, the less importance we give to them.
Hence, in his 'Value' chapter of the *Introduction*, Bentham has 'propin-
quity or remoteness' as one of the measures of value (IV, 2), and this is
correct with respect to the descriptive psychology which he is laying out
at this point as to how things are actually valued; that is, the effect they
actually have on us. However, Sidgwick does not think that this is
rational, even from a self-interested, egoistic, point of view. What we
should be doing is displaying no time-preference at all since the value of
a state of affairs should be the same at whatever time it happens. (We can
discount for certainty, and, normally, the further off in the future something is, the less certain it is; however, this is a different reason for discount and one mentioned separately by Bentham.) So now we get
another crack in the system, in the things which were held together in the
earlier utilitarian psychology. This time it is between self-interest on the
one hand and motivation by apparent pain and pleasure on the other.
Even if we think that there is nothing to self-interest other than one's own
happiness, and even if we think that happiness consists of no more than
pleasure and the absence of pain, it will still be the case that the motivating force of apparent pleasures and pains may not be in our interest.
Even if we anticipate future pleasures and pains correctly, we discount
them more than we should; hence we act too much on the appearances
and not in our long-term interest.

The importance of this in the present context is the following. If we
are to be rational egoists, then we should not follow the immediately

motivating force of apparent pain and pleasure. But sanctions are what actually motivate; that is, what actually explain the psychology of action. Hence we cannot identify sanctions and rational self-interest. Hence, contrary to first appearances, an account of the sanctions of utilitarianism will not be the same as an account of the coincidence of self-interest and benevolence. It may be remembered that when Sidgwick introduces the question at the start of the chapter, he talks of how 'a man must have a certain impulse to do what is reasonable'. Just so. However, now we find that to be 'reasonable' includes both rational self-interest and also rational benevolence. Someone may indeed need an impulse in addition to the mere perception of what is reasonable. But, if so, this applies equally to both ways of being reasonable. That is, we need an additional impulse to be rational in terms of our self-interest as much as we do in terms of benevolence. The question of sanctions, therefore, if it applies at all, applies equally to both. We have to explain how people are able to be self-interested as much as we have to explain how they are able to be benevolent. The question of sanctions for being rational cannot therefore be the same question as whether there are self-interested reasons to be moral.

Sidgwick is quite explicit that in this he is following Butler, another past philosopher with whom he is in conversation. It is Butler who, as Sidgwick quite explicitly says, gives him the dualism. It is Butler who, before Sidgwick, brings out how people fail to act in their own interests. Butler is a clergyman giving sermons. We might therefore expect him to criticise self-interested actions and tell people instead to be moral. However, perhaps surprisingly, he criticises them instead for failures of self-interest. As he puts it in his *First Sermon*, 'men in fact and as often contradict that *part* of their nature which respects *self*, and which leads them to their *own private* good and happiness; as they contradict that *part* of it which respects *society, and* tends to the *public* good'. In other words, we are equally deficient in both of Sidgwick's ultimate reasons (rational self-interest; rational benevolence), and both equally need strengthening.

Such strengthening might be by political action, again forming a political solution to a moral (or here it would be better to say a rational) problem. Hence in contemporary road-traffic legislation, the government may act to control speed and safety of vehicles, aiming at the benevolent effect on the other people who would otherwise be damaged by the driver's actions. But it can equally intervene politically, not allowing people to drive without their seat belts, or motorcyclists to ride without crash helmets, thus instituting sanctions designed to make people more concerned with their own future happiness, making them more rational egoists. Similarly for the areas of indirect legislation or advertising, whether public or private. The pictures of the far-off famine make the pain of others vivid and real and so motivate people into benevolent action. Similarly, the far-off sufferings of lung cancer may be made vivid and real to present-day smokers, motivating them to act in their own interests. Again it is not the fact of the pleasure and pain which motivates, or gives the sanction, but, rather, how it is made apparent to someone at a particular time and place.

We can, of course, as philosophical or psychological commentators, attempt to give an external description of how it works. An explanation, that is, of how it is possible for people to be rationally benevolent or rationally self-interested; of how the show is kept on the road. Even if we disagree with Mill's remark that 'desiring a thing and finding it pleasant, aversion to it and thinking of it as painful, are phenomena entirely inseparable' (*Utilitarianism*, IV), we may still recognise that there is a close connection between finding something painful and the desire to avoid it. We recognise that pains are naturally motivating and that the prospect of pain gives reasons for action. So, if we are concerned about how the show is kept on the road, how people may be successfully self-interested or how a society is able to reproduce itself in its moral culture, then the explanation will be helped if we can see how doing the moral things is generally pleasurable and not doing them is generally painful, just as we can explain the physical reproduction of society by the pleasures of conception.

This may take us some way. However, pains and, even more, the more amorphous so-called pleasures are merely some motives among others. So if we are explaining performance by motivation they will only take us, at best, part of the way. We might expect a general fit, but there is no reason why it should be perfect. This, as we have seen, is also true of prudence, so that following our immediate desires or our anticipations of pleasure or pain may be anything but prudent. Pain is, no doubt, an important signal. When our hand on the stove pains us, it is likely also to be the case that not just pleasure but also self-interest recommends its removal. However, when Emily Brontë returned from a walk during which she had been bitten by a rabid dog and cauterised the wound with the red-hot poker from the fire, she was behaving prudentially and rationally. It was a heroic piece of self-interested self-sacrifice.

Psychology is a normative science. We interpret people not just as believers of the true but also as lovers of the good. In understanding (or interpreting) them, we understand how they would justify themselves both to themselves and also to us; that is, what they would recognise as ultimate reasons for action. As such, Sidgwick's (and before him Butler's) claim seems to me to be highly plausible; namely that we recognise as such ultimate reasons that something is in someone's interest (or leads to their happiness) and also that something is in the general interest (or benefits someone else). An action is explained if it is shown how it avoids pain either for the agent or for someone else. It explains it by providing a recognisable justification. As Sidgwick says, 'happiness appears to be a reasonable end ... if I can say of any action that it makes me happier, it seems that no further account need be given of my doing it' (I, 59).

Hence we have the dualism, but here in a different way from anything directly connected with sanctions. If 'sanctions' just means what can (rationally) motivate me, then either of these considerations can provide sanctions, that is, reasons. It is not that one of them (say, self-interest) forms a particular kind of sanction different from the other. On the other hand, as we have seen, if 'sanction' means an immediate anticipation of pleasure and pain, then neither reason will directly follow from such sanctions. So the asymmetry which seems to be implied in Sidgwick's last chapter between self-interest and benevolence drops away. Indeed, it has to drop away if the dualism of practical reason is to assume the important and final position in which Sidgwick places it, for such dualism necessarily depends upon the equal weight and value of each of its two elements.

An important part of the answer to why we are able to be moral may be no better than that people are able to see the truth (or, alternatively, that the truth is constituted by what people are able to see). Take the comparable question of how we are able to do mathematics; that is, what keeps the mathematical show on the road. This is both a theoretical and a practical question. It is the question of how we can go on continuing the series correctly, adding plus 2 in the same way as everyone else when we reach 115,326; 115,328; 115,330 ... However, it is also the question how, having 4 plus 1 bolts, we know that we need 3 plus 2 nuts to fasten them. We could explore how the size or workings of the brain enables us to do this. We could look at education and initial conditioning. But in the end we may get a no more interesting answer than that it is true that 115,326 plus 2 is 115,328 or that it is true that $4 + 1 = 2 + 3$. It is a truth which, as it happens, we are able to see; or, alternatively, we see it, and truth here is constituted by what we are able to see.

In the more obviously practical, or moral, case it need be no different. The show is kept on the road; people are able to tell that they should not torture innocent children. Again, no doubt, we could investigate brain power or initial education. But, again, the best answer may be the banal one that we can do it because it is true and we are able to see it; or, again, alternatively, the truth here is constituted by what we are able to see. That is, we are motivated to be moral by seeing that what is moral motivates. Of course if we thought that only self-interest motivates, then we would have to see how this could give a reason for so-called 'moral' actions, for keeping promises, not torturing babies and so on. However, this is not Sidgwick's problem, for Sidgwick thinks that as well as the ultimate rationality of self-interest there is the ultimate rationality of benevolence. Hence I have a direct practical reason to be moral; and having a practical reason is, for Sidgwick, to have something which motivates. So all that is required for him to be able to explain why we are able to be moral is to show, firstly, that this reason can be demonstrated to be true and, secondly, that it is a truth of which people are aware.

Sidgwick does, I take it, prove both of these things in *The Methods of Ethics*. He does it by relating utilitarianism (or rational benevolence) in two different ways to the doctrines which he labels intuitionism. We have what he calls philosophical intuitionism, the high-level intuitive (or rational) principles epitomised by Kant. From these it follows (or so, at least, Sidgwick thinks) that 'the good of any one individual is of no more importance, from the point of view ... of the Universe than the good of any other' (VII, 382). That is, good should be considered impartially; hence the rationality of benevolence, the rationality of considering another's good as neither more nor less important than your own. However, if we stop here this might be like a truth provable by professors but unavailable to the multitude. Hence the importance of his examination of what he calls common-sense morality; that is the morality of the people. Sidgwick himself is concerned to point out in the second edition preface that this morality is also his own, but the next point follows whether Sidgwick is part of the government house elite or part of the rabble. This point is that for Sidgwick this common-sense morality can be systematised and reduced so that it reveals what he calls 'unconscious utilitarianism'. Hence the rabble, the people (all of us), do know the right (utilitarian) morality in our everyday or common-sense morality about not killing our granny and so on. Sidgwick considers common-sense morality a kind of intuitionism, and the book of the *Methods of Ethics* called 'Intuitionism' is mainly an account and systematisation of common-sense morality. So, for him, both kinds of intuitionism converge on utilitarianism. To show this was, after all, the great feat of the *Methods*. In the present context it means that everyone, whether philosopher with knowledge of the form of the good or slave boy scribbling in the sand, knows the right answer to the question about what they ought to do. And this knowledge is sufficient for both to keep the show on the road. No other sanctions are required.

Of course if the good is dual and possibly diverges, then there may be problems. Earlier Sidgwick himself points out, while he is talking about sanctions, that the sanctions mentioned by Mill and Bentham may diverge. For example, the deliverances of my conscience may not coincide with Bentham's 'popular or moral sanction'; that is, with what public opinion presses on me as right conduct. Divergence is possible and divergence causes practical problems. But any set of things sufficiently simple to be useful in either explanation or justification will cause such occasional practical problems. General lack of divergence is all that is necessary for the set to be practically useful. Sometimes (because of divergence) there may be a hiccup but, in general, this pair of fundamental reasons for action works perfectly well and works much better than any suggested alternative. This includes the alternative of using just one member of the dualism.

This is, if we treat it as a practical problem, a question of what we should do. However, Sidgwick, because his dualism is of reason rather than of sanctions, thinks that the problem here is more theoretical than practical. For him there cannot be two equally fundamental but possibly competing reasons. He thinks that such possible conflict is fatal to the theoretical enterprise of truly describing practical reason; possible conflict reduces cosmos to chaos. However, I do not myself see that this is a serious, let alone fatal, problem. Early in the *Methods* Sidgwick says that 'no doubt it is a postulate of practical reason, that it must be consistent with itself: and hence we have a strong predisposition to reduce any two methods to unity' (I, 66). However, he also adds 'that it is a special object of the present work to avoid all hasty and premature reconciliations'. At the end, hundreds of pages later, we might think that he had successfully avoided being hasty and that it was time for reconciliation. Yet it is just here that he thinks that he fails in reconciliation.

As a consequentialist ethic, the problem is not that the two reasons give quite different reasons for action, quite different ways of thinking about our intentions when acting. Providing the right thing is done whichever way we think about it, this would not be a problem on a consequentialist ethic. The problem is that, according to how we think about it, different consequences could follow. Otherwise it would just be like two different ways of thinking about the same thing. To take an analogy, if it could be shown that the two ultimate principles necessarily fitted together, then it would be like analytical geometry. If you have a fundamental algebraic turn of mind, then you can understand these truths algebraically, understanding figures like circles and ellipses in terms of their equations. Alternatively, if you have a geometrical turn of mind, you can think of these figures as what the algebra is really about, understanding the equations in terms of the diagrams. There is a dualism of perception, but it can also be shown mathematically that, whichever way we choose to see it, we will come up with corresponding results. So, applying the analogy, some may see our actions in terms of enlightened self-interest, some in terms of rational benevolence. However, whichever way they are seen, corresponding truths with respect to action will emerge. The same behaviour ensues, even if it is given different descriptions.

From Plato, geometry may be taken to be a description of ideas (of the ideal world). The actual figures we draw in the sand fall short. In ethics, what is described is doubly ideal. It is, again, ideas, ideas which our actual actions in the sands of this world fail to realise. Yet these ideas are here themselves the ideal, the good, the goal; not something which describes the actual world but, rather, something to which we would wish the actual world to conform. We may rationally see that this ideal contains the good for someone of their interests being met. We may also see that the good contains the impersonal meeting of such goods. This practically ideal world, this best of all possible worlds, therefore contains both. We may, I think, consistently suppose that this best of all possible worlds contains both relative and non-relative goods (the good from my perspective and the good in itself). Then, for some-one in this best of all possible worlds, it would be like my description of analytical geometry. There, whether you think algebraically or geo-metrically, you get the same truths. Here, whether you think in terms of relative or non-relative goods, you think that the same things are good. You can pursue your own good, you can pursue the impartial good; what you pursue is the same. This is the best of all possible worlds. The actual world is not like this. However, the actual world would be a better world if doing the right thing (objectively, or non-relatively, speaking) did not involve self-sacrifice. It would be a better world if realising your self in pursuit of your fundamental interests resulted in an objectively better world also for others.

These points can be put in both a relativised and a non-relativised way. If we just think of goods from no point of view, then it will be trivially better (in terms of such non-relativised goods) if we can move from a situation in which someone sacrifices herself to produce good to others to a situation in which she can produce the same good to others without sacrificing herself. For we have the same good for others but more good for her; hence more good overall. However, this is too simple. We are concerned not with a world which is best in every dimension but, rather, with the best possible world; and for this some sacrifice may be unavoidable. The utilitarian theory of government imposes potential costs on some (by threatening punishment) for the greater good of others. As people are, a perfect system of punishment is the best that is possible.

This is one way in which this account is too simple. It also is too simple in a more fundamental manner. For if we just consider goods from no particular point of view, we miss the centre of Sidgwick's dualism, which necessarily depends upon considering goods in a relativised manner; that is, we have to consider how John's good gives John a special reason to act, over and above it just being a good (otherwise Sidgwick's refutation of egoism would apply). So we need as well a relativised way of making the point that self-sacrifice is not involved in the best of all possible worlds. In fact this can also be done. It is better for me if I can move from a world with a certain amount of good for me to a world in which there is more good for me and the same good for others. Not just better in itself, but better for me in a relativised way. Furthermore, it is also good for me that what is good for me is not incompatible with what is good for all. Conflict in goals is not just bad; it is also bad for me—bad in a relativised way.

Reconciliation between the two fundamental ultimate reasons for action would be premature if it can be shown that they are both ultimate, that both provide fully explicable motivation, or (in this sense) sanctions. Take, for example, the so-called 'golden rule', the precept that you should do unto others as you would that they should do unto you. This was the kind of moral truth which Sidgwick would have learned at his mother's knee, at church, and in school, being enshrined in the Anglican catechism. 'What is thy duty towards my neighbour?', the catechist asked, and the reply to be learned was 'My duty towards my neighbour is to love him as myself and to do to all men as I would they should do unto me.' However, this is not just an Anglican eccentricity. Behind it stand similar statements in both the Old and New Testaments of the Bible. Nor is this just a foible of Western civilisation. As was observed in the anthropologically conscious seventeenth century, tenets like this were discovered to hold in widely dispersed cultures. Pufendorf, for example, noted it in both Confucius and the Incas. So this worked for them as a posteriori evidence of an a priori, or purely rational, truth. Something seemingly held by all people and without any evidence of acquisition by cultural diffusion must be a truth of reason, perceivable by people just because they were rational animals. Otherwise put, it was inscribed in the hearts of men by the hand of God, so explaining how people without biblical revelation might know the moral truth. It was therefore part of natural law. Indeed, even that highly eccentric proponent of the new natural law, Thomas Hobbes, said that all the laws of nature had been, as he put it, 'contracted into one easy sum, intelligible, even to the meanest capacity; and that is, *Do not that to another, which thou wouldest not have done to thy selfe*' (*Leviathan*, ch. 15). That Hobbes, as Sidgwick points out in *The Methods of Ethics*, is here propounding the rules to be followed for self-preservation just makes the universality of this dictum even more striking.

So here we have a good example of an obvious moral or rational precept; something which gives good reasons for action; something which in the seventeenth century and earlier was inscribed by the hand of God but which later became enshrined in one of its aspects in the high gospel of pure practical reason. Sidgwick himself says (in his 'Sanctions' chapter) that 'I find that I undoubtedly seem to perceive, as clearly and certainly as I see any axiom in Arithmetic or Geometry, that it is "right" and "reasonable", and "the dictate of reason" and "my duty" to treat every man as I think that I myself ought to be treated in precisely similar circumstances' (I, 470). However, what does this intuitively compelling moral truth tell us to do? It contains two points, one about the nature of the good and one about its distribution. On the nature of the good, it gives as a practical rule for identification that the good is things which you would want; or, alternatively, that the bad is things that you would not want. Things that you would not have people do to you are bad things. So this identifies the good (or, alternatively, the bad). Then the other point is about distribution. It is that you should impartially promote this good in others as well as yourself; or not impose this bad on others any more than you would on yourself.

The impartial bit is obvious, recognisably moral, and receives expression in the requirement that moral maxims be universalised. It goes with Sidgwick's 'universal reason', his rational, impartial, benevolence. However, what is equally interesting here is the other part, that is the part which identifies the good rather than saying how it should be distributed. This is done by what people find good for themselves; that is, it is done by the relativised sense of the good in which my good provides me with particular reasons for me to act. Unless the good is identified in this way, then there is no point talking about how you would that people should act unto you. In other words, the formula only makes sense if it is already supposed that we naturally have self-interested reasons for action; that we naturally understand that our good gives a reason to us. Only if we understand this can we use it as a means of identifying the good, and only if we can identify the good can the impartial distribution point operate. Hence, to have the familiar moral rationality of what Sidgwick calls universal reason, we also need the rationality of what Sidgwick calls individual reason. As he says, they are both rational principles.

Sidgwick's problem is not that both of these ultimate principles are deep, but that they do not necessarily converge. They are neither necessarily connected in themselves nor, at least for Sidgwick, is it a necessary truth that there is a god who, as a necessary attribute of his goodness, connects them. So they possibly diverge. However, because these are truths of practical rather than speculative reason, this should not matter. The two may diverge. All this shows is that, if they do, we are not in the best of all possible worlds. The two may diverge, but it can still be true that they ought not to diverge. In the best possible world they would coincide. A god, or indeed any legislator who was both benevolent and omnipotent, would bring this about.

That is how I think that Sidgwick should have got out of his problem. I think that he could have taken the problem on its own terms and still solved it. However, this is not what he actually did. Instead he noted the strong objections to his startling confession of failure and rewrote the chapter. He dropped the famous ending, and so dropped the explicit declaration of failure. But he still held, as he puts it in the second edition preface, that the main discussion of this chapter was 'indispensable to the completeness of the work'. He still quite explicitly affirms both principles and indeed for the first time he describes it as a 'dualism of the practical reason' (II, xii). So the main offensive claim is maintained, and maintaining it means, at least in Sidgwick's eyes, that the hoped-for cosmos of duty is still a chaos and the main project is still a failure.

In fact, these changes make this point more conspicuous. For, as Sidgwick also claims in this new second edition preface, the main misunderstanding he wished to avoid was that his intention was to argue for only one of his three methods (utilitarianism) at the cost of the other two (egoism and intuitionism). With intuitionism, it is true, he effects a reconciliation. However, Sidgwick wishes to make it quite clear that with egoism he has effected neither a reconciliation nor a defeat. Egoism is still fully in play along with utilitarianism, and hence the dualism of reason, or failure to unify.

Other changes which Sidgwick did not remark on in his new preface make this more conspicuous. The last chapter in the first edition is Chapter 6 of Book IV, the book entitled 'Utilitarianism'. So, as such, it looks like the end of the account of utilitarianism, the end of the account of what looks like Sidgwick's preferred doctrine. This is helped by its title, the title I adopted for this paper, 'The sanctions of utilitarianism'. As such it seems to fit neatly after the preceding chapter, 'The method of utilitarianism', which comes after 'The proof of utilitarianism'. The whole forms an exposition and defence of utilitarianism similar to Mill's in content although superior in argumentative texture.

For the second edition Sidgwick dropped this. The last chapter was moved out of Book IV and given a heading of its own, of equal weight to the headings of the previous four books. It now forms a separate end to the whole work rather than being the end of the utilitarian Book IV. He might have called it 'Book V'; instead he calls it 'Concluding Chapter'. He also gives it a new title. Instead of the title referring to utilitarianism, used by this paper, it is henceforth called 'The mutual relations of the Three Methods'. Hence, as he says in the new preface, he makes quite specific that his interest in this chapter is in the relation between utilitarianism and egoism, not in further defence or discussion of utilitarianism itself. This all necessarily makes any tension involved in the dualism more fully embedded in Sidgwick's overall project, even if perhaps not quite so superficially apparent in the closing words. He holds, as I remarked, that the chapter, and hence the statement of the dualism, was 'indispensable'.

What else might he have done? If he had instead carried on with the utilitarian tack implied by its original heading, he could have dropped the talk of 'sanctions'; indeed, simply dropped the chapter. Then the work would truly have been the defence of utilitarianism which it was naturally read as being and which, in spite of Professor Sidgwick's protests, it still obviously is. The work would not then have ended with the word 'failure'. Instead it would have ended with the concluding words of the previous chapter, which Sidgwick left unchanged from first edition to last. Here he notes the 'stress which Utilitarians are apt to lay on social and political activity of all kinds, and the tendency which Utilitarian ethics has always shown to pass into politics'. He notes, that is, the stress on what I earlier called the political solution of moral problems. And then he concludes the chapter, and it might have been the book, by saying, 'A sincere Utilitarian, therefore, is likely to be an eager politician: but on what principles his political action ought to be determined, it scarcely lies within the scope of this treatise to investigate.' A fine conclusion, and one which makes way for Professor Sidgwick's next treatise, *The Elements of Politics*.

Sanctions in Bentham, Mill,
and Sidgwick[1]

ROGER CRISP

ROSS HARRISON DESERVES THE THANKS of Sidgwick scholars not only for organising this centennial conference, but for his stimulating enquiry into Sidgwick's views on an issue which was considered of great importance by the classical utilitarians of the eighteenth and nineteenth centuries, but which has received little direct attention during this century—the sanctions of morality. What I think is particularly instructive in his discussion is its demonstration that enquiry into the nature of sanctions can illuminate other more well-trodden areas, such as the dualism of practical reason and Sidgwick's attitude to commonsense morality.

It seems churlish to criticise, but such is the way of philosophy; so let me try to niggle a little. First, I want to suggest that Mill was more of a precursor of Sidgwick, and less a follower of Bentham, than Ross suggests. Mill is not a psychological hedonist, nor indeed a psychological egoist of any stripe. He does think that all desire is for the perceived greatest balance of the agent's pleasure over pain, but for Mill 'desire' is a technical term reserved for that particular—admittedly very common—motivation. He allows for weakness of will: 'Men often, from infirmity of character, make their election for the nearer

---

[1] References to Mill's *Utilitarianism* give chapter and paragraph number; those to Sidgwick's *The Methods of Ethics* are to the seventh edition; and the reference to the *Memoir* is A. and E. M. Sidgwick, *Henry Sidgwick, A Memoir* (London: Macmillan, 1906).

Proceedings of the British Academy, **109**, 117–122. © The British Academy 2001.

good, though they know it to be the less valuable; and this no less when the choice is between two bodily pleasures, than when it is between bodily and mental' (*Utilitarianism*, 2.7); and for self-sacrifice: 'Unquestionably it is possible to do without happiness; ... it often has to be done voluntarily by the hero or the martyr, for the sake of something which he prizes more than his individual happiness' (*Utilitarianism*, 2.15). So the need to explain the sanctions of self-interest, how—in the case of weakness at least—to convert motivation by will (see *Utilitarianism*, 4.11) into motivation by desire, is as salient for Mill as it is for Sidgwick.

The dualism of practical reason is a doctrine about the sources of reasons. As Ross notes in his concluding remarks, Sidgwick recognised that his dualism need not result in any irresoluble practical conflict, though of course he did think it did so result. Ross also makes what I think is a very important point: anyone who attempts to move to an impartial principle on the back of an account of welfare which itself seems to assume that the agent has reason to pursue that welfare for herself may find herself in danger of a dualism. Here, then, is another place in which I think Mill anticipates Sidgwick. Not only does Mill offer us an account of welfare which implicitly appeals to our desire for pleasure, or our recognition that it is worth pursuing for ourselves, but his proof explicitly makes that appeal. Further, the final paragraph of the chapter on sanctions in *Utilitarianism* is a straightforward appeal to the rationality of self-interest: given the strength of each human being's desire to be in unity with others, and the higher pleasure to be taken in that unity, the best prospect of one's own happiness in a well-organised society will be found in pursuing the happiness of all. And, we assume, Mill meant that to be another argument in favour of impartiality, in certain circumstances at least.

The fact that he ends Chapter 3 like that, incidentally, suggests that he is, on this matter at least, less exact and coherent than either Bentham or Sidgwick. Mill does not keep clearly separate the psychological question—what might motivate a utilitarian agent?—from the ethical or normative question—why *should* anyone feel obliged to act in accordance with utilitarianism? (To be fair, neither does Sidgwick: when he says, in the passage quoted by Ross, '[M]any persons will still feel that, after all, it has not really been shown why a man should be a consistent Utilitarian', it might have been clearer had he written 'would' rather than 'should'.)

My second niggle concerns Bentham (I'll come to Sidgwick at the end). Or rather it concerns what Ross says about Bentham. Ross attempts to draw a distinction between Bentham on the one hand, and Mill and Sidgwick on the other, relating to the scope of sanctions. The moral problem is how to motivate people to do what will promote the greatest happiness overall, when they are, to a large extent, out to promote their own greatest happiness. According to Ross, Bentham provides a 'political solution' to this moral problem. Well, that is of course correct as far as it goes. But it is not as if Bentham's sanctions don't provide other, non-political—that is, non-legislative—sources of motivation. An obvious example is the moral sanction itself—that is, the opinion of others—which Mill himself made so much of in accounting for the peculiar institution of morality itself. Right across the board, I see Bentham, Mill, and Sidgwick engaged in both the moral and the political enterprises in roughly the same way. None of them sees himself as a mere commentator on a machine baking cakes, but as an adviser to cake-makers—politicians, and anyone else who will listen—on how to build the best machines for the purposes of political or social, or indeed personal, morality, or how to tinker with the steam-driven items we find ourselves already working with, in the hope of improving their productivity.

Finally, some remarks on Sidgwick on sanctions. Ross's sympathetic and dispassionate account of Sidgwick's intuitionism is, I think, absolutely spot on. But I don't think that this intuitionism, when bolted on to Sidgwick's motivational internalism, is sufficient, by Sidgwick's own lights, to explain how and why we are able to be moral.

'Motivation' is a slippery term in contemporary ethics, and many writers appear ready to take views on it without spelling out exactly what they take it to mean. There is a clear distinction to be made, for example, between motivation which is sufficient for action, and that which is not, as well as between motivation as some kind of introspectively discernible felt impulse, and motivation understood counterfactually (to be motivated to phi is to be in a state such that, were countervailing motivations absent, one would phi). I suspect that most contemporary motivational internalists accept a counterfactual version of a story about insufficient motivations. That is, if I believe that it is wrong to phi, I may indeed phi, but my state is such that, were counter-vailing motivations absent, I would not—indeed, would deliberately abstain.

So even to state a half-decent version of motivational internalism seems to require a good account of counterfactuals in this area which, as far as I know, we do not have. But Sidgwick does not run into this problem at all, since he understands motivation as an introspectible 'impulse'. Having stated his view on p. 34 of the seventh edition, he begins the next section as follows: 'I am aware that some persons will be disposed to answer all the preceding argument by a simple denial that they can find in their consciousness any such unconditional or categorical imperative as I have been trying to exhibit.' And, rather than offer us a counterfactual story, Sidgwick goes on to suggest—in a way that cannot help but remind one of Hume on the calm passions—that if these persons will only examine themselves carefully enough many of them will find that their denial of the moral impulse is really nothing more than an expression of hostility to deontological ethics.

Interestingly, Sidgwick does not insist that this *must* be the case, which raises another distinction between versions of motivational internalism: the empirical thesis that a person who judges that it is wrong to phi will be motivated not to phi, which can be turned quite happily into a generalisation not to be falsified by the odd exception, and a conceptual version of the same view, which would be in trouble with a single counter-example. I suspect that many modern internalists take the conceptual line; could it be that Sidgwick is here taking the empirical?

To return to sanctions, and the sufficient/insufficient distinction. Sidgwick does indeed say, as Ross quotes him: 'when I speak of the cognition or judgement that "X ought to be done"—in the stricter ethical sense of the term ought—as a "dictate" or "precept" of reason ... I imply that in rational beings as such this cognition gives a motive or impulse to action' (7, 34). That this is not a watering-down of inter-nalism to the thin Korsgaardian gruel that even the toughest externalist can imbibe is made clear by the implication which immediately follows, that every human being capable of making a moral judgement is *eo ipso* a rational being. But note the form in which this implication is embedded: 'in human beings, of course, this is only one motive among others which are liable to conflict with it, and is not always— perhaps not usually—a predominant motive'. In other words, the moral motivation that follows upon acceptance of a moral judgement is very likely to be sadly insufficient for the action required, and that leaves plenty of room to explain how and why sufficient motivation can be provided—that is, plenty of room for discussion of sanctions.

Unlike John Mackie, Ross is disappointed by Sidgwick's pessimism, and suggests that he might have kept to the plan of the first edition, left out the pessimism, and—Aristotle-like—referred the reader to his works on politics to explain how sanctions might provide a resource for bringing about an overlap between morality and self-interest.

The pessimism was certainly in line with Sidgwick's mood when he completed the book. In February 1874 he wrote of it: 'It bores me very much, and I want to get it off my hands before it makes me quite ill' (*Memoir*, 287), and the authors of the memoir say that the depression that affected Sidgwick in the final stages of writing a book was 'painful'. But even had he been more cheerful I think Sidgwick would have resisted Ross's suggestion. Sidgwick almost certainly thought that any project to make human beings to any great degree more impartial than they are would be self-defeating. The maxim of prudence could not be made consistent with that of rational benevolence:

> There are very few persons, however strongly and widely sympathetic, who are so constituted as to feel for the pleasures and pains of mankind generally a degree of sympathy at all commensurate with their concern for wife or children, or lover, or intimate friend: and if any training of the affections is at present possible which would materially alter this proportion in the general distribution of our sympathy, it scarcely seems that such a training is to be recommended as on the whole felicific. (7, 502)

Further, as long as any gap remained between self-interest and impartial morality, and self-interest was of equal rational standing with impartial morality, Sidgwick would not have found himself able, in a work on philosophy, to hide that fact. Sidgwick allows that it would be 'a most valuable contribution to the actual happiness of mankind' to come up with a machine to close the gap; but he is not, he says, 'now considering what a consistent Utilitarian will try to effect for the future' (7, 499). Sidgwick really thought the utilitarian philosophical project had run into the ground, and his integrity as a philosopher would not have permitted him to hide that all-important fact. And, because he was no utilitarian, he could not have accepted that there was any overriding moral reason to do so either.